Chronology and documentary handbook of the state of Minnesota

Seal of the State of Minnesota

CHRONOLOGY AND DOCUMENTARY HANDBOOK OF THE STATE OF

MINNESOTA

ROBERT I. VEXLER

State Editor

WILLIAM F. SWINDLER

Series Editor

1978 OCEANA PUBLICATIONS, INC./Dobbs Ferry, New York

Library of Congress Cataloging in Publication Data

Main entry under title
Chronology and documentary handbook of the State of Minnesota.

(Chronologies and documentary handbooks of the States; 23)
Bibliography: p.
Includes index.
SUMMARY: Includes a chronology of events in Minnesota from 1648 to 1977, a biographical directory of prominent citizens, and selected documents.
1. Minnesota—History—Chronology. 2. Minnesota—Biography. 3. Minnesota—History—Sources. [1. Minnesota—History] I. Vexler, Robert I. II. Series.
F606.5.C47 977.6'002'02 78-15236
ISBN 0-379-16148-6

Manufactured in the United States of America

TABLE OF CONTENTS

ACKNOWLEDGMENT

Special recognition should be accorded Melvin Hecker, whose research has made a valuable contribution to this volume.

Thanks to my wife, Francine, in appreciation of her help in the preparation of this work.

Thanks also to my children, David and Melissa, without whose patience and understanding I would have been unable to devote the considerable time necessary for completing the state chronology series.

Robert I. Vexler

INTRODUCTION

This projected series of Chronologies and Documentary Handbooks of the States will ultimately comprise fifty separate volumes - one for each of the states of the Union. Each volume is intended to provide a concise ready reference of basic data on the state, and to serve as a starting point for more extended study as the individual user may require. Hopefully, it will be a guidebook for a better informed citizenry - students, civic and service organizations, professional and business personnel, and others.

The editorial plan for the Handbook series falls into six divisions: (1) a chronology of selected events in the history of the state; (2) a short biographical directory of the principal public officials, e.g., governors, Senators and Representatives; (3) a short biographical directory of prominent personalities of the state (for most states); (4) the first state constitution; (5) the text of some representative documents illustrating main currents in the political, economic, social or cultural history of the state; and (6) a selected bibliography for those seeking further or more detailed information. Most of the data found in the present volume, in fact, have been taken from one or another of these references.

The current constitutions of all fifty states, as well as the federal Constitution, are regularly kept up to date in the definitive collection maintained by the Legislative Drafting Research Fund of Columbia University and published by the publisher of the present series of Handbooks. These texts are available in most major libraries under the title, Constitutions of the United States: National and State, in two volumes, with a companion volume, the Index Digest of State Constitutions.

Finally, the complete collection of documents illustrative of the constitutional development of each state, from colonial or territorial status up to the current constitution as found in the Columbia University collection, is being prepared for publication in a multi-volume series by the present series editor. Whereas the present series of Handbooks is intended for a wide range of interested citizens, the series of annotated constitutional materials in the volumes of Sources and Documents of U. S. Constitutions is primarily for the specialist in government, history or law. This is not to suggest that the general citizenry may not profit equally from referring to these materials; rather, it points up the separate purpose of the Handbooks, which is to guide the user to these and other sources of authoritative information with which he may systematically enrich his knowledge of this state and its place in the American Union.

William F. Swindler
Series Editor

Robert I. Vexler
Series Associate Editor

L'Etoile du Nord/
The Star of the North

State Motto

CHRONOLOGY

1648-59 Winter. Pierre Radisson and Groseilliers were the first known white explorers who passed the winter with the Sioux Indians in the Mille Lacs region.

1671 The Sieur de Lasson read a proclamation urging the French claim to all territory in the region of the Great Lakes. He made this claim at Sault Sainte Marie before representatives of 14 Indian nations.

1673 Louis Joliet and Pere Marquette explored the upper part of the Mississippi River.

1679 Daniel Greysolon, Sieur du Lhut (Duluth), explored the area of the land from the head of Lake Superior to Mille Lacs. He planted a standard bearing the arms of King Louis XIV of France in what later became a Sioux village. The Sieur du Lhut was an agent for a company of Canadians who sought to establish a series of trading posts on the Great Lakes.

1680 Father Louis Henepin, a Franciscan friar, explored part of the region of Minnesota acting as an agent for the Sieur de la Salle. Henepin discovered and named the Falls of St. Anthony.

1694 Le Sueur, who had been involved in trading with the Indians along the upper Mississippi as early as 1684, established a trading post on Isle Pelée (Prairie) in the Mississippi River between Hastings and Red Wing.

1700 Le Sueur erected Fort L'Huillier at the point where the Blue Earth and Le Sueur rivers meet.

1762 The Sieur de la Perriere, who served as an agent of the French government, constructed a fortified post, Fort Beauharnois, on the west bank of Lake Pepin. This post was to be the headquarters for missionaries, as well as a trading post. In addition it was a starting-point for expeditions in search of the so-called "western sea."

Spain received western Minnesota from France as part of the grant of land given in return for Spain's support in the Seven Years' War and the French and Indian War.

1763 By the Treaty of Versailles France transferred the eastern portion of Minnesota (that is the territory east of the Mississippi) to Great Britain.

1766 Jonathan Carver of Connecticut visited Minnesota.

1783 By the Treaty of Paris ending the American Revolutionary War Great Britain ceded the eastern portion of Minnesota to the United States.

1784 Congress accepted Virginia's surrender of her title to western lands which included Minnesota.

1787 The eastern part of Minnesota became a part of the Northwest Territory through the Ordinance of 1787. Britain still maintained possession of the area in violation of the Treaty of Paris of 1783. Her citizens still did some trading there and continued to do so until 1796.

1800 France received the western part of Minnesota from Spain.

1803 The United States received title to western Minnesota as part of the Louisiana Purchase from France.

1805-06 Under orders from President Thomas Jefferson Zebulon M. Pike led an exploring expedition which reached Leech Lake. He took formal possession of Minnesota for the United States. In addition Pike made a treaty with the Sioux Indians for military reservations, receiving one tract nine miles square at the mouth of the St. Croix River, and another tract of about 100,000 acres at the point where the Minnesota and Mississippi rivers meet.

1818 October 20. Great Britain ceded Northern Minnesota to the United States.

1819 Lieutenant-Colonel Henry Leavenworth established a military post at the point where the Mississippi and Minnesota rivers meet.

Michigan Territory was extended west to the Mississippi River.

November 3. McMinn County was created, with Athens as its county seat. It was named for Joseph McMinn who fought in the Revolutionary War, was a member of the Tennessee Senate and was the fifth governor of Tennessee.

1820 General Lewis Cass, governor of the Territory of Michigan, led an exploring expedition in an attempt to discover the source of the Mississippi. He was satisfied that the source was located in Lake Cass, which was named in his honor.

Construction of Fort St. Anthony, which was renamed Fort Snelling in 1824 in honor of its builder and commander Col. Josiah Snelling.

1823 February 4. Rankin County, with its seat at Brandon, was established. It was named for Christopher Rankin, a member of the Mississippi territorial legislature and the constitutional convention as well as a Representative from Mississippi.

Major Stephen Harriman Long made very extensive explorations of the Minnesota and the Red River valleys.

Giacomo Constantio Beltrami, an Italian travellor and political refugee, searched for the source of the Mississippi.

The first steamboat to travel the Mississippi River reached Fort Snelling from St. Louis.

1832 Henry Rowe Schoolcraft, who traveled with Lewis Cass's expedition, traced the Mississippi River from Lake Cass to Lake Itasca.

1836 Wisconsin Territory was created, including all of Minnesota.

1837 July 29. Governor Henry Dodge of Wisconsin signed a treaty with the Chippewa Indians at St. Peters. The Chippewas gave up their titles to almost all their lands east of the Mississippi River.

September 29. Joel R. Poinsett signed a treaty with the Sioux Indian chiefs at Washington, D. C., whereby they gave up almost all of their lands west of the Missipsippi River.

1838 Iowa Territory was created, including the western part of Minnesota (that portion west of the Mississippi River).

1848 August 26. A convention was held at Stillwater, where measures were passed for the creation of a separate territorial government. Henry Hastings Sibley was sent to Congress as a delegate of "Wisconsin Territory."

1849 March 3. Minnesota was established as a separate territory. Slavery was prohibited.

March 19. President Zachary Taylor appointed Alexander Ramsey, a Whig from Pennsylvania the first territorial governor of Minnesota. He served in this capacity until 1853.

September 3. The first territorial legislature met at St. Paul.

October 27. The following counties were established: Benton, Dakota, Itasca, Ramsey, and Washington. Benton, with its county seat at Foley, was named for Thomas Hart Benton, Senator and Representative from Missouri. Dakota, with Hastings as its seat, was named for the Dakota Indian tribe. Itasca, with its seat at Grad Rapids, was organized March 6, 1857. Ramsey, which was organized March 31, 1851, effective September 1, 1851, with its seat at St. Paul, was named for Alexander Ramsey, first territorial governor of Minnesota, later Mayor of St. Paul, second governor of Minnesota, Senator from Minnesota and Secretary of War in the administration of President Rutherford B. Hayes.

Washington County, organized March 31, 1851, effective September 1, 1851, with its seat at Stillwater, was named for George Washington, commander of all Continental Armies and first President of the United States.

James Madison Goodhue began publication of the first territorial newspaper, the <u>Minnesota Pioneer</u>, at St. Paul.

1850 Population of Minnesota Territory: 6,077.

1851 February 13. The University of Minnesota was created by a territorial act. Instruction did not begin until 1868, and the first degrees were granted in 1873.

March 31. Chisago County was created, effective September 1, 1851, and organized January 1, 1852, with its seat at Center City.

July 23. Indian Commissioner Luke Lea and Governor Alexander Ramsey negotiated two treaties with the Sioux Indians whereby the Sioux turned over most of their land in Minnesota to the United States and thus opening most of the land in the territory west of the Mississippi to settlement.

1852 March 6. Hennepin County, with Minneapolis as its seat, was established. It was named for Louis Hennepin, Roman Catholic friar who explored the Great Lakes region with the Cavalier de La Salle in 1679 and the upper Mississippi Region in 1680.

1853 March 5. The following counties were created: Blue Earth, Fillmore, Goodhue, Le Sueur, Nicollet, Rice, Scott, and Sibley. Blue Earth has its seat at Mankato. Fillmore, with its seat at Preston, was named for Millard Fillmore, Vice President and President of the United States.

Goodhue, with Red Wing as its county seat, was named for James Madison Goodhue who published the first newspaper in Minnesota, the Minnesota Pioneer in 1849. Le Sueur, with its seat at Le Center, was named for Pierre Charles Le Sueur, trader, miner, fur trader, who built a fort on Prairie Island, near Red Wing, Minnesota.

Nicollet County, with St. Peter as its county seat, was named for Joseph Nicolas Nicollet, a French mathematician who emigrated to New Orleans in 1832. He made exploring trips up the Mississippi to its source at Lake Itasca. Rice County, with its seat at Faribault, was named for Henry Mower Rice, a delegate from Minnesota as well as U. S. Senator.

Scott County, with its county seat at Shakopee, was named for Winfield Scott, who fought in the War of 1812 and was commander-in-chief of the U. S. Army from 1841 to 1861. Sibley, with its seat at Gaylord, was organized March 2, 1854. It was named for Henry Hastings Sibley, a delegate from the Minnesota Territory and the first governor of Minnesota.

Willis Arnold Gorman, Democrat, became governor of Minnesota Territory in which post he served until 1857.

1854 February 23. Houston and Winona Counties were were established. Houston, with Caledonia as its county seat, was named for Samuel Houston, second and fourth president of the Texas Republic as well as Representative from and governor of Tennessee and Senator from and governor of Texas. Winona, with its seat at Winona, was named for Winona, a Dakota Indian woman.

Hamline University was founded and chartered at St. Paul.

1855 February 20. The following counties were established: Brown, Carver, Dodge, Faribault, Freeborn, Mower, Renville, St. Louis, Stearns, Steele, Todd, and Wright.

Brown, with its seat at New Ulm, was organized February 11, 1856, and was named for Joseph Renshaw Brown, Secretary of the Minnesota territorial council, chief clerk and member of the Minnesota house of representatives. Carver, with Chaska as its seat, was named for Jonathan Carver, a captain in the French and Indian War, who signed an Indian treaty in 1767.

Dodge, with its seat at Manterville, was named for Henry Dodge, first and fourth governor of the Wisconsin territory and Senator from Wisconsin. Faribault, organized February 23, 1856, with Blue Earth as its seat, was named for Jean Baptiste Faribault, a French-Canadian fur trader who was an agent in the northwest for the American Fur Company.

Freeborn, organized March 6, 1857, with its seat at Albert Lea, was named for William

Freeborn, who served in the Minnesota territorial legislature. Mower, organized March 1, 1856, with its seat at Austin, was named for John E. Mower, a member of the Minnesota territorial legislature and the house of representatives.

Renville, with Olivia as its county seat, was named for Joseph Renville, who was part Sioux. He served as interpreter for Lt. Pike's conference with the Sioux in 1805-06 and later led the Sioux warriors against the U. S. frontier. He aided in the translation of the Bible in the Sioux language.

St. Louis County, with its seat at Duluth, was named for Saint Louis, King Louis IX of France. Stearns, with its county seat at St. Cloud, was organized March 3, 1855, and was named for Charles Thomas Stearns, a member of the Minnesota territorial legislature. Steele, with Owatonna as its seat, was named for Franklin Steele, a member of the first board of regents of the University of Minnesota.

Todd, with its county seat at Long Prairie, was organized March 1, 1856. It was named for John Blair Smith Todd, a graduate of the United States Military Academy at West Point, who fought in the Seminole and Mexican Wars and was a member of the Dakota territorial legislature and speaker of the house.

Wright County, organized March 2, 1855, with its seat at Buffalo, was named for Silas Wright, sixteenth governor of New York and Representative and Senator from New York.

1856 February 23. Meeker County, with its seat at Litchfield, was created. It was named for Bradley B. Meeker, associate justice of the Minnesota Supreme Court.

February 25. Morrison and Sherburne Counties were established. Morrison, with its seat at Little Falls, was named for Allan Morrison, a fur trader and member of the Minnesota territorial legislature. Sherburne, with its seat at Elk River was named for Moses **Sherburne,** associate justice of the supreme court of the Minnesota territory.

March 1. McLeod and Pine Counties were created. McLeod, with its seat at Glencoe, was named for Martin McLeod, a member of the Minnesota territorial legislature and president of the Minnesota territorial council. Pine County has its seat at Pine City.

1857 February 13. Isanti County, with its seat at Cambridge, was named for the Izatys Indians.

March. Ink-pa-du-ta, a Sioux, led his band to massacre the settlers at Spirit Lake.

May 23. The following counties were established: Aitkin, Anoka, Carlton, Cottonwood, Crow Wing, Jackson, Martin, Mille Lacs, Murray, Nobles, Pipestone, and Rock. Aitkin, with its county seat at Aitkin, was named for William Alexander Aitkin, a fur trader who worked for the Fond du Lac department of the American Fur Company. Anoka, with Anoka as its seat, was named for the Indian word meaning "on both sides of the river."

Carlton, with its seat at Carlon, was named for Reuben B. Carlton, a member of the Minnesota Senate. Cottonwood, with its seat at Windom, was named for the Cottonwood River. Crow Wing has its seat at Barinerd.

Jackson County, with its seat at Jackson, was named for Henry Jackson, one of the first merchants of St. Paul, and a member of the first territorial legislature. Martin, with Fairmont as its county seat, was named for Henry Martin, an early settler. Mille Lacs, with its seat at Milaca, is the French term for "a thousand lakes."

Murray County, with its seat at Slayton, was named for William P. H. Murray, a member of the Minnesota territorial legislature as well as a member of the state house of representatives and the state senate. Nobles, with its county seat at Worthington, was named for William H. Nobles, a member of the Minnesota territorial legislature, who also discovered Nobles Pass through the Rocky Mountains.

Pipestone County, with Pipestone as its seat, was organized January 27, 1879 Rock, with its county seat at Laverne, was organized March 5, 1870.

July. The state constitutional convention met and found it difficult to organize because it was evenly divided between the Democrats and the Republicans. The conference committes produced two identical constitutions.

October. The state constitution was adopted almost unanimously by the people.

Samuel Medary, Democrat, became governor of the territory in which post he served until 1858.

St. John's University was founded and chartered at Collegeville.

1858 March 8. Douglas County, with its seat at Alexandria, was created. It was named for Stephen Arnold Douglas, Senator and Representative from Illinois.

March 13. Kanabec County was established, with Mora as its seat.

March 18. The following counties were created: Becker, Clay, Otter Trail, and Wilkin. Becker, with its seat at Detroit Lakes, was named for George Loomis Becker, a brigadier general in the U. S. Army, Mayor, of St. Paul, member of the Minnesota legislature and of the state railroad and warehouse commission.

Clay County, with Moorhead as its seat, which was originally Breckinridge County, until its name was changed on March 6, 1862, was named for Henry Clay. He was Senator from Kentucky and Secretary of State in the administration of President John Quincy Adams.

Otter Trail County, with Fergus as its seat, was organized March 16, 1868. Wilkin, with Breckinridge as its seat, was named for Alexander Wilkin, secretary of the Minnesota Territory, who also served in the Civil War and was killed at the battle of Tupelo, Mississippi on July 14, 1864. It was originally called Toombs County, being changed to Andy Johnson County in 1862 and then to its present name on March 6, 1868.

March 20. Kandigohi County was established, with its seat at Willmar.

May 11. Minnesota was admitted to the Union as the 32nd state.

May 24. Henry Hastings Sibley, Democrat, became the first governor of the state in which post he served until January 2, 1860.

July 20. Polk County was created, with Crookston as its seat. It was named for James Knox Polk, 11th President of the United States.

Winona State College was established at Winona.

1860 Population: 172,023.

January 2. Alexander Ramsey, Republican, became governor of the state and served in the office until his resignation on January 10, 1863.

February 25. Watonwan County, with its seat at St. James, was created and named for the Watonwan River.

1862 February 6. Redwood County was established, with Redwood Falls as its seat.

February 20. The following counties were created: Big Stone, Chippewa, Pope, Stevens, and Traverse. Big Stone has its seat at Ortonville. Chippewa, with its seat at Montevideo, was named for the Chippewa Indian Tribe.

Pope, with Glenwood as its county seat, was named for John Pope, a graduate of the U. S. Military Academy at West Point. He explored the Rocky Mountains and served in the Civil War. Stevens, with its seat at Morris, was named for Isaac Ingalls Stevens, a graduate of the U. S. Military Academy at West Point, who fought in the Mexican War, was first territorial governor of Washington and a delegate from the territory of Washington, and served as a major general in the Civil War.

Traverse County has its seat at Wheaton.

April 24. Kittson County, with its seat at Hallock, was established and organized on February 25, 1879. It was named for Norman Wolfred Kittson, a member of the Minnesota territorial legislature and mayor of St. Paul. It was originally called Pembina County until its name was changed on March 9, 1878.

August 18. Chief Little Crow led a Sioux uprising in Minnesota as a result of a delay in paying the Indians their annual allowance. The Sioux were decisively defeated by Col. Henry Hastings Sibley on September 23.

September 26. Over 2,000 Indians were surrounded and captured. Chief Little Crow and seevral companions fled beyond the Missouri.

Gustavus Adolphus College was founded at St. Peter.

1863 Col. Henry H. Sibley led an expedition which drove the hostile Indians further away from the settlers. General Alfred Sully eventually drove the Indians beyond the Missouri and ended the war.

July 10. Henry A. Swift, Republican, beoamo governor of the state and served in that capacity until January 11, 1864.

1864 January 11. Stephen Miller, Unionist and Republican, who had been elected in 1863, became governor of Minnesota and served in the office until January 8, 1866.

The University of Minnesota was established by an act of the legislature.

1865 February 23. The state legislature ratified the 13th Amendment to the United States Constitution.

1866 January 8. William Rogerson Marshall, Republican, became governor of the state and served until January 9, 1870.

February 28. Beltrami County was established, with Bimidji as its county seat. It was named for Giacomo Constantino Beltrami, an explorer who traveled up the Mississippi River and discovered one of its principal sources.

May 1. Lincoln County, with its seat at Ivanhoe, was created. It was named for Abraham Lincoln, 16th President of the United States.

Carlton College was founded and chartered at Northfield.

1867 January 17. The state legislature ratified the 14th Amendment to the United States Constitution.

Mankato State College was established at Mankato.

1868 March 6. Grant and Lyon Counties were established. Grant, with its county seat at Elbow Lake, was named for Ulysses Simpson Grant, a major general in the U. S. Army during the Civil War and later 18th President of the United States. Lyon, with Marshall as its seat, was named for Nathaniel Lyon, a graduate of the U. S. Military Academy at West Point, who was killed in the Civil War at the battle of Wilson's Creek, Missouri on August 10, 1861.

1869 First classes were held at the University of Minnesota, Minneapolis.

Augsburg College was founded at Minneapolis, and St. Cloud State College was established.

1870 Population: 439,706.

January 9. Horace Austin, Republican, who had been elected in 1869, became governor of the state and served in the gubernatorial office until January 7, 1874.

January 13. The state legislature ratified the 15th Amendment to the United States Constitution.

February 18. Swift County, with its seat at Benson, was created. It was named for

Henry Adoniram Swift, member of the Minnesota Senate and lieutenant-governor and governor of Minnesota.

1871 March 6. Lac Qui Parle and Yellow Medicine Counties were established. Lac Qui Parle, with its county seat at Madison, was named for the French term "the lake which talks." Yellow Medicine County, with Granite Falls as its seat, was named for the Yellow Medicine River.

Bethel College was founded and chartered at St. Paul.

1874 January 7. Cushman Kellog Davis, Republican, who had been elected in 1873, became governor and served in this capacity until January 7, 1876.

March 9. Cook County, with its seat at Grand Marais, was established. It was named for Michael Cook a state senator. He served in the Civil War and was killed at the battle of Nashville in 1864.

St. Olaf College was established at Northfield.

1876 January 7. John Sargent Pillsbury, Republican, who had been elected in 1875, became governor of Minnesota. He served in the office until January 10, 1882.

1879 February 25. Marshall County, with its seat at Warren, was created. It was named for William Rainey Marshall, who served in the Civil War and was fifth governor of Minnesota.

December 10. Alexander Ramsey was appointed Secretary of War by President Rutherford B. Hayes. Ramsey assumed his office as a member of the cabinet on December 12, 1879.

1880 Population: 780,773

1881 February 17. Norman County, with Ada as its seat, was established. It was named for Norman Wolfred Kittson, a member of the Minnesota territorial legislature and mayor of St. Paul.

March 5. William Windom was appointed Secretary of the Treasury by President James A. Garfield. He assumed his office as a member of the cabinet on March 8.

1882 January 10. Lucius Fairchild Hubbard, Republican, who had been elected in 1881, became governor of Minnesota and served in the office until January 5, 1887.

1885 February 20. Olmsted County, with Rochester as its seat, was created. It was named for David Olmsted, president of the first territorial legislature of Minnesota and first mayor of St. Paul.

The College of St. Thomas was founded and chartered at St. Paul.

1886 The Minneapolis College of Art and Design was established.

1887 January 5. Andrew Ryan McGill, Republican, who was elected in 1886, became governor of the state and served in this capacity until January 9, 1889.

1887 Moorhead State College was founded.

1888 A college of medicine, now the College of Medicine and Surgery at the University of Minnesota, was founded.

1889 January 9. William Rush, Republican, who was elected in 1888, became governor of the state and served in the gubernatorial office until January 4, 1893.

March 5. William Windom was appointed Secretary of the Treasury by President Benjamin Harrison. He assumed his office as a member of the cabinet on March 7, 1889 and served until his death on January 24, 1891.

William W. Mayo and his two sons established the Mayo Clinic at Rochester.

1890 Population: 1,310,283.

Rich iron-ore deposits were discovered in the Mesabi range.

1891 Concordia College was established at Moorhead.

1892 June 7-11. The Republican National Convention met in Minneapolis where it nominated President Benjamin Harrison as its presidential candidate and Whitelaw Reid of New York as its vice presidential candidate.

The first iron ore was shipped from the Mesabi range.

1893 January 4. Knute Nelson, Republican, who had been elected in 1892, became governor of Minnesota and served in this capacity until January 31, 1895.

Concordia College was established at St. Paul.

1894 February 28. Roseau County was established with its seat at Roseau.

September 1. A forset fire destroyed the towns of Hinkley and Sandstone, killing 418 persons.

1895 January 31. David Marston Clough, Republican, who had been elected in 1894, became governor of the state and served in the office until January 2, 1899.

1896 December 24. Red Lake County was created, with its seat at Red Lake Falls.

St. Paul Seminary was founded and chartered at St. Paul.

1898 October. A band of Chippewa Indians rose up at Leech Lake. Federal troops were brought in to put down the uprising and were successful.

1899 January 2. John Lind, Democrat-Populist, who had been elected in 1898, became governor of the state and served in office until January 7, 1901.

1900 Population: 1,751,394.

1901 January 7. Samuel R. Van Sant, Republican, who had been elected in 1900, became governor of Minnesota and served in office until January 4, 1905.

1902 December 20. Clearwater County was created, with Bagley, as its county seat.

The Duluth Branch of the University of Minnesota was established as a state normal school.

1905 January 4. John Albert Johnson, Democrat, who had been elected in 1904, became governor of the state. He served in office until his death on September 21, 1909.

The College of St. Benedict was established at St. Joseph.

1906 December 19. Koochiching County, with its seat at International Falls, was established.

December 27. Mahnomen County was created, with Mahnomen as its seat.

1907 The College of St. Theresa was founded and chartered at Winona.

1909 March 9. Todd County, with its seat at Long Prairie, was created. It was named for John Blair Smith Todd, an Indian trader in Dakota, delegate from Dakota Territory, and member of the Dakota territorial legislature as well as its speaker.

September 21. Adolph Olson Eberhart, Republican, became governor of the state upon the death of Governor John Albert Johnson. Eberhart served until January 5, 1915, having been subsequently elected.

1910 Population: 2,075,708

November 23. Pennington County was created, with Thief River Falls as its county seat. It was named with Edmund Pennington, superintendent, general manager and president of the St. Paul and Sault Ste Marie Railroad Company.

1911 The state legislature abolished the death penalty.

The first shipment of iron ore left the Cuyuna Range.

1912 June 10. The state legislature ratified the 17th Amendment to the United States Constitution.

June 11. The state legislature ratified the 16th Amendment to the United States Constitution.

The College of St. Scholastica was established at Duluth and St. Mary's College at Winona.

1913 The College of St. Benedict was founded at St. Joseph.

1915 January 5. Winfield S. Hammond, Democrat, who was elected in 1914, became governor of Minnesota. He served in the office until his death on December 30, 1915.

December 30. Lieutenant Governor Joseph A. A. Burnquist, Republican, became governor of Minnesota upon the death of Winfield S. Hammond. He was subsequently elected and served until January 5, 1921.

1916 July 19-21. The National Convention of the Prohibition Party met at St. Paul, where it nominated Frank Hanly of Indiana for President and Ira D. Landrith of Massachusetts for Vice President.

A large steel mill went into operation at Duluth.

1918 October 13-15. A disastrous forest fire occurred in Carlton and St. Louis Counties, killing more than 400 persons and destroying property over $25,000,000.

1919 January 17. The state legislature ratified the 18th Amendment to the United States Constitution.

September 8. The state legislature ratified the 19th Amendment to the United States Constitution.

Bimidji State College was founded and chartered.

1920 Population: 2,387,125.

1921 January 5. Jacob A. O. Preus, Republican, who had been elected in 1920, became governor of the state and served until January 6, 1925.

1922 November 28. Lake of the Woods County, with Baudette as its seat at Baudette, was created.

WLB (now KUOM), an educational radio station, owned by the University of Minnesota, became the first licensed station in the state.

1923 October 10. The state legislature ratified the 21st Amendment to the United States Constitution.

WDGY became the first commercial station broadcasting from Minneapolis.

1924 June 19. The National Convention of the Farmer-Labor-Progressive Party was held at St. Paul where it nominated Duncan MacDonald for President of the United States and William Bouck for Vice President. The two candidates stepped aside on July 10. William Z. Foster and Benjamin Gitlow then became the nominees for president and vice president respectively.

1925 January 6. Theodore Christianson, Republican, who had been elected in 1924, became governor of the state, and served until January 6, 1931.

February 16. Frank B. Kellogg was appointed Secretary of State by President Calvin Coolidge. Kellogg assumed his office as a member of the cabinet on March 5, 1925.

1929 March 5. James Dewitt Mitchell was appointed Attorney General by President Herbert Hoover. Mitchell assumed his office as a member of the cabinet on March 6, 1929

1930 Population: 2,563,953.

1931 January 6. Floyd B. Olson, Farmer-Labor, who had been elected in 1930, became governor of Minnesota. He served in the office until his death on August 22, 1936.

1933 January 12. The state legislature ratified the 20th Amendment to the United States Constitution.

1936 August 22. Lieutenant Governor Hjalmar Peterson, Farmer-Labor, became governor of Minnesota upon the death of Governor Floyd B. Olson. Peterson served in the gubernatorial office until the end of the term on January 4, 1937.

1937 January 4. Elmer A. Benson, Farmer-Labor, who had been elected in 1936, became governor of the state and served in the office until January 2, 1939.

1939 January 2. Harold E. Stassen, Republican, who had been elected in 1938, became governor of the state. He served in office until his resignation on April 27, 1943.

1940 Population: 2,792,300.

1943 April 27. Lieutenant Governor Edward J. Thye, Republican, became governor of Minnesota upon the resignation of Governor Harold E. Stassen. Thye was subsequently elected and served until January 8, 1947.

1944 The Farmer-Labor Party joined the Minnesota Democratic Party to form the Democratic-Farmer-Labor Party.

1947 January 8. Luther W. Youngdahl, Republican, who had been elected in 1946, became governor of Minnesota . He served in the office until his resignation September 27, 1951.

1948 KSTP-TV began broadcasting from Minneapolis as the first television station in the state.

1950 Population: 2,982,483.

1951 September 27. Lieutenant Governor C. Elmer Anderson, Republican, became governor upon the resignation of Governor Luther W. Youngdahl. Anderson was subsequently elected and served until January 5, 1955.

1953 August 15. President Dwight D. Eisenhower signed a bill which transferred from federal to state courts jurisdiction in regard to Indians.

1955 January 5. Orville L. Freeman, Democratic-Farmer-Labor, who had been elected in 1954, became governor of the state. He served in office until January 2, 1961.

A taconite processing plant opened at Silver Bay to extract iron from low-grade taconite ore.

1956 May 2. The General Conference of the Methodist Church, meeting in Minneapolis, demanded the abolition of all racial segregation in the Methodist Churches.

1960 Population: 3,413,864.

1961 January 2. Elmer L. Andersen, Republican, who had been elected in 1960, became governor of the state. He served for the two-year term and then for three months of the succeeding four-year term until March 25, 1963, when the disputed election of 1962 was decided by a court in favor of his opponent Karl Rolvaag.

January 21. Orville L. Freeman became Secretary of Agriculture in the Cabinet of President John F. Kennedy.

January 31. The state legislature ratified the 23rd Amendment to the United States Constitution.

1963 February 27. The state legislature ratified the 24th Amendment to the United States Constitution.

March 25. Karl F. Rolvaag, Democratic-Farmer-Labor, became governor of the state. He had opposed Elmer Anderson in the 1962 election. Anderson had been declared the winner and was inaugurated in January, 1963. However, Rolvaag challenged the election results, and the Minnesota Supreme Court subsequently ruled that Rolvaag was the winner by 91 votes. Rolvaag served in the office of governor until January 2, 1967.

1964 The citizens of Minnesota ratified a state constitutional amendment assuring that taconite products wil not be taxed at a higher rate than on other business products for 25 years.

1965 May 6. 13 people died in a tornado which struck Minneapolis.

1966 May 20. Governor Karl F. Rolvaag signed a measure which provided for reapportionment of the Minnesota House and Senate.

1967 January 2. Harold Le Vander, Republican, who had been elected in 1966, became governor of the state and served in the office until January 4, 1971.

February 10. The state legislature ratified the 25th Amendment to the United States Constitution.

1970 Population: 3,804,971.

1971 January 4. Wendell R. Anderson, Democratic-Farmer-Labor, who had been elected in 1970 became governor of the state. He was reelec-reelected to a second term on November 5, 1974.

March 23. The state legislature ratified the 26th Amendment to the United States Constitution.

Voyageurs National Park was established in the state consisting of 214,128 acres.

Southwest Minnesota State College was established at Marshall.

1972 May 12. Governor Wendell R. Anderson activated 715 National Guardsmen to deal with anti-Vietnam war protestors at the University of Minnesota in Minneapolis.

1973 February 8. The state legislature ratified the Equal Rights Amendment to the United States Constitution.

1976 May 4. U. S. District Judge Edward J. Devitt ordered the Revere Mining Company of Silver Bay and its parent firms to pay fines totaling over $1,000,000 as a result of its polluting Lake Superior.

July 15. Senator Walter F. Mondale of Minnesota received the Democrat Party's nomination for Vice President of the United States at the party's national convention in New York City.

November 2. Senator Walter F. Mondale was elected Vice President of the United States along with Jimmy Carter who was elected President.

December 29. Rudolph George Perpich became governor of the state. He succeeded Governor Wendell R. Anderson who resigned to take the United States Senate seat of Walter F. Mondale, who was elected Vice President of the United States. Mondale's resignation and Anderson's appointment by Governor Perpic became effective December 30.

1977 April 1. Robert L. Herbst, commissioner of the state Department of Natural Resources, was confirmed in his appointment as assistant secretary of interior for fish and wildlife.

August 1. AFL-CIO United Steel Workers Union members went on strike in the state The strike was settled on December 16.

October 23. President Jimmy Carter made a brief stop in Minneapolis on his return from Los Angeles, California to Washington, D. C. in order to pick up Senator Hubert H. Humphrey who was returning to the capital after a two month treatment for inoperable cancer.

BIOGRAPHICAL DIRECTORY

The selected list of governors, United States Senators and Members of the House of Representatives for Minnesota, 1835-1977, includes all persons listed in the Chronology for whom basic biographical data was readily available. Older biographical sources are frequently in conflict on certain individuals, and in such cases the source most commonly cited by later authorities was preferred.

ALDRICH, Cyrus
Republican
b. Smithfield, R. I., June 18, 1808
d. Minneapolis, Minn., October 5, 1871
U. S. Representative, 1859-63

ALEXANDER, John Grant
Republican
b. Texas Valley, N. Y., July 16, 1893
U. S. Representative, 1939-41

ANDERSEN, Elmer L.
Republican
b. Chicago, Ill., June 17, 1909
Governor of Minnesota, 1961-63

ANDERSEN, Herman Carl
Republican
b. Newcastle, Wash., January 27, 1897
U. S. Representative, 1939-63

ANDERSON, Clyde E.
Republican
Governor of Minnesota, 1951-55

ANDERSON, Sidney
Republican
b. Zumbrota, Minn., September 18, 1881
d. Minneapolis, Minn., October 8, 1948
U. S. Representative, 1911-25

ANDERSON, Wendell R.
Democrat-Farmer-Labor
b. St. Paul, Minn., February 1, 1933
Governor of Minnesota, 1971-

ANDRESEN, August Herman
Republican
b. Newark, Ill., October 11, 1890
d. Bethesda, Md., January 14, 1958
U. S. Representative, 1925-33, 1935-58

ARENS, Henry
Farmer-Labor
b. Westphalia, Germany, November 21, 1873
d. Jordan, Minn., October 6, 1963
U. S. Representative, 1933-35

AUSTIN, Horace
Republican
Governor of Minnesota, 1870-74

AVERILL, John Thomas
Republican
b. Alma, Maine, March 1, 1825
d. St. Paul, Minn., October 3, 1889
U. S. Representative, 1871-75

BALDWIN, Melvin Riley
Democrat
b. near Chester, Vermont, April 12, 1838
d. Seattle, Wash., April 15, 1901
U. S. Representative, 1893-95

BALL, Joseph Hurst
Republican
b. Crookston, Minn., November 3, 1905
U. S. Senator, 1940-42, 1943-49

BEDE, James Adam
Republicam
b. North Eaton Township, Ohio, January 13, 1856
d. Duluth, Minn., April 11, 1942
U. S. Representative, 1903-09

BENSON, Elmer Austin
b. Appleton, Minn., September 22, 1895
U. S. Senator, 1935-36
Governor of Minnesota, 1937-39

BERGLAND, Bob
Democrat
b. July 31, 1928
U. S. Representative, 1971-

BERNARD, John Toussant
Farmer-Labor
b. Bastia, Isle of Corsica, France, March 6, 1893
U. S. Representative, 1837-39

BLATNIK, John Anton
Democrat
b. Chisholm, Minn., August 17, 1911
U. S. Representative, 1947-

BOEN, Haldor Erickson
People's Party
b. Sondre Aurdal, Valders, Norway, January 2, 1851

d. Aurdal Township, Minn., July 23, 1912
U. S. Representative, 1893-95

BUCKLER, Richard Thompson
Farmer-Labor
b. near Oakland, Ill., October 27, 1865
d. Crookston, Minn., January 23, 1950
U. S. Representative, 1935-43

BUCKMAN, Clarence Bennet
Republican
b. Doylestown, Pa., April 1, 1851
d. Battle Creek, Mich., March 1, 1917
U. S. Representative, 1903-07

BURNQUIST, Joseph A. A.
Republican
b. Dayton, Iowa, July 21, 1879
d. January 12, 1961
Governor of Minnesota, 1915-21

CARSS, William Leighton
Farmer-Labor
b. Pella, Iowa, February 15, 1865
d. Duluth, Minn., May 31, 1931
U. S. Representative, 1919-21 (Independent), 1925-29 (Farmer-Labor)

CASTLE, James Nathan
Democrat
b. Shefford, Province of Quebec, Canada, May 23, 1836
d. Stillwater, Minn., January 2, 1903
U. S. Representative, 1891-93

CAVANAUGH, James Michael
Democrat (Minnesota/Montana)
b. Springfield, Mass., July 4, 1823
d. Leadville, Colorado, October 30, 1879
U. S. Representative, 1858-59 (Minnesota), (Territorial Delegate), 1867-71 (Montana)

CHRISTGAU, Victor Laurence August
Republican
b. Dexter Township, near Austin, Minn., September 20, 1894
U. S. Representative, 1929-33

CHRISTIANSON, Theodore
Republican
b. near Lac Qui Parle Township, Minn., September 12, 1883

d. Dawson, Minn., December 10, 1948
Governor of Minnesota, 1925-31
U. S. Representative, 1933-37

CLAGUE, Frank
Republican
b. Warrensville, Ohio, July 13, 1865
d. Redwood Falls, Minn., March 25, 1952
U. S. Representative, 1921-33

CLAPP, Moses Edwin
Republican
b. Delphi, Ind., May 21, 1851
d. at his country home "Union Farm," near Accotink, Va., March 6, 1929
U. S. Senator, 1901-17

CLOUGH, David N.
Republican
b. Lyme, N. H., December 27, 1846
d. August 28, 1924
Governor of Minnesota, 1895-99

COMSTOCK, Solomon Gilman
Republican
b. Argyle, Maine, May 9, 1842
d. Moorhead, Minn., June 3, 1933
U. S. Representative, 1889-91

DAVIS, Cushman Kellogg
Republican
b. Henderson, N. Y., June 16, 1838
d. St. Paul, Minn., November 27, 1900
Governor of Minnesota, 1874-76
U. S. Senator, 1887-1900

DEVITT, Edward James
Republican
b. St. Paul, Minn., May 5, 1911
U. S. Representative, 1947-49

DUNNELL, Mark Hill
Republican
b. Buxton, Maine, July 2, 1823
d. Owatonna, Minn., August 9, 1904
U. S. Representative, 1871-83, 1889-91

EBERHART, Adolph O.
Republican
Governor of Minnesota, 1909-15

EDDY, Frank Marion
Republican

b. Pleasant Grove, Minn., April 1, 1856
d. St. Paul, Minn., January 13, 1929
U. S. Representative, 1895-1903

EDGERTON, Alonzo Jay
Republican
b. Rome, N. Y., June 7, 1827
d. Sioux Falls, S. D., August 9, 1896
U. S. Senator, 1881

ELLSWORTH, Franklin Fowler
Republican
b. St. James, Minn., July 10, 1879
d. Minneapolis, Minn., December 23, 1942
U. S. Representative, 1915-21

FLETCHER, Loren
Republican
b. Mount Vernon, Maine, April 10, 1833
d. Atlanta, Georgia, April 15, 1919
U. S. Representative, 1893-1903, 1905-07

FRASER, Donald Mackay
Democrat-Farmer-Labor
b. Minneapolis, Minn., February 20, 1924
U. S. Representative, 1963-

FREEMAN, Orville Le.
Democrat-Farmer-Labor
b. Minneapolis, Minn., May 9, 1918
Governor of Minnesota, 1955-61
U. S. Secretary of Agriculture, 1961-69

FRENZEL, William E.
Republican
b. July 31, 1928
U. S. Representative, 1971-

FURLOW, Allen John
Republican
b. Rochester, Minn., November 9, 1890
d. Rochester, Minn., January 29, 1954
U. S. Representative, 1925-29

GALE, Richard Pillsbury
Republican
b. Minneapolis, Minn., October 30, 1900
U. S. Representative, 1941-45

GALLAGHER, William James
Democrat
b. Minneapolis, Minn., May 13, 1875
d. Rochester, Minn., August 13, 1946

U. S. Representative, 1945-46

GILFILLAN, John Bachop
Republican
b. Barnet, Vermont, February 11, 1875
d. Minneapolis, Minn., August 19, 1924
U. S. Representative, 1885-87

GOODWIN, Godfrey Gummer
Republican
b. near St. Peter, Minn., January 11, 1873
d. Washington, D. C., February 16, 1933
U. S. Representative, 1925-33

HAGEN, Harold Christian
b. Crookston, Minn., November 10, 1901
d. Washington, D. C., March 19, 1957
U. S. Representative, 1943-45 (Farmer-Labor), 1945-55 (Republican)

HALL, Darwin Scott
Republican
b. Mound Prairie, Wis., January 23, 1844
d. near Olivia, Minn., February 23, 1919
U. S. Representative, 1889-91

HALL, Osee Matson
Democrat
b. Conneaut, Ohio, September 10, 1847
d. St. Paul, Minn., November 26, 1914
U. S. Representative, 1891-95

HALVORSON, Kittel
Farmers Alliance - Prohibitionist
b. Telemarken, Norway, December 15, 1846
d. Havana, N. Dak., July 12, 1936
U. S. Representative, 1891-93

HAMMOND, Winfield Scott
Democrat
b. Southboro, Mass., November 17, 1863
d. Clinton, La., December 30, 1915
U. S. Representative, 1907-15
Governor of Minnesota, 1915

HARRIES, William Henry
Democrat
b. near Dayton, Ohio, January 15, 1843
d. Seattle, Wash., July 23, 1921
U. S. Representative, 1891-93

HEATWOLE, Joel Prescott
Republican

b. Waterford, Mills., Ind., August 22, 1856
d. Northfield, Minn., April 4, 1910
U. S. Representative, 1895-1903

HOWARD, Guy Victor
Republican
b. Minneapolis, Minn., November 28, 1879
d. Minneapolis, Minn., August 20, 1954
U. S. Senator, 1936-37

HUBBARD, Lucius F.
Republican
b. Troy, N. Y., January 26, 1836
d. St. Paul, Minn., February 5, 1913
Governor of Minnesota, 1882-87

HUMPHREY, Hubert Horatio, Jr.
Democrat
b. Wallace, S. Dak., May 27, 1911
d.
U. S. Senator, 1949-64
Vice President of the United States, 1965-69
U. S. Senator, 1971-78

JOHNSON, Dewey William
Farmer-Laborite
b. Minneapolis, Minn., March 14, 1899
d. Minneapolis, Minn., September 18, 1941
U. S. Representative, 1937-39

JOHNSON, John Albert
b. St. Peter, Minn., July 28, 1861
d. September 21, 1909
Governor of Minnesota, 1905-09

JOHNSON, Magnus
Farmer-Laborite
b. near Karlstadt in Ed Paris, Varmland, Sweden, September 19, 1871
d. Litchfield, Minn., September 13, 1936
U. S. Senator, 1923-25
U. S. Representative, 1933-35

JUDD, Walter Henry
Republican
b. Rising City, Nebr., September 25, 1898
U. S. Representative, 1943-63

KARTH, Joseph Edward
Democrat
b. New Brighton, Minn., August 26, 1922
U. S. Representative, 1959-

KELLER, Oscar Edward
Republican
b. Helenville, Wis., July 30, 1878
d. St. Paul, Minn., November 21, 1927
U. S. Representative, 1919-27

KELLOGG, Frank Billings
Republican
b. Potsdam, N. Y., December 22, 1856
d. St. Paul, Minn., December 21, 1937
U. S. Senator, 1917-23
U. S. Secretary of State, 1925-29

KIEFER, Andrew Robert
Republican
b. Marienborn, Duchy of Hesse Darmstadt, near City of Mainz, on the Rhine, Germany, May 25, 1832
d. St. Paul, Minn., May 1, 1904
U. S. Representative, 1893-97

KING, William Smith
Republican
b. Malone, N. Y., December 16, 1828
d. Minneapolis, Minn., February 24, 1900

KINGSBURY, William Wallace
Democrat
b. Towanda, Pa., June 4, 1828
d. Tarpon Springs, Florida, April 17, 1892
U. S. Representative (Territorial Delegate), 1857-58

KNUTSON, Coya Gjesdal
Democrat-Farmer-Labor
b. Edmore, N. Dak., August 22, 1912
U. S. Representative, 1955-59

KNUTSON, Harold
Republican
b. Skien, Norway, October 20, 1880
d. Wadena, Minn., August 21, 1953
U. S. Representative, 1917-49

KVALE, Ole Juulson
Farmer-Laborite
b. near Decorah, Iowa, February 6, 1869
d. near Otter Trail Lake, Minn., September 11, 1929
U. S. Representative, 1923-25 (Republican), 1925-29 (Farmer-Laborite)

KVALE, Paul John
Farmer-Laborite

b. Orfordville, Wis., March 27, 1896
d. Minneapolis, Minn., June 14, 1960
U. S. Representative, 1929-39

LANGER, Odin
Republican
b. Minneapolis, Minn., January 5, 1913
U. S. Representative, 1959-71

LARSON, Oscar John
Republican
b. Uleaborg, Finland, May 20, 1871
d. Duluth, Minn., August 1, 1957
U. S. Representative, 1921-25

LEVANDER, Harold
Republican
Governor of Minnesota, 1967-71

LIND, John
Democrat
b. Kanna, Sweden, March 25, 1854
d. Minneapolis, Minn., September 18, 1930
U. S. Representative, 1887-93 (Republican)
Governor of Minnesota, 1898-1900 (Democrat)
U. S. Representative, 1903-05 (Democrat)

LINDBERGH, Charles Augustus
Republican
b. Stockholm, Sweden, January 20, 1859
d. Crookston, Minn., May 24, 1924
U. S. Representative, 1907-17

LUNDEEN, Ernest
Farmer-Laborite
b. near Beresford, S. Dak., August 4, 1878
d. in airplane crash, Lovettsville, Va., August 31, 1940
U. S. Representative, 1917-19 (Republican), 1933-37 (Farmer-Laborite)
U. S. Senator, 1937-40 (Farmer-Laborite)

MAAS, Melvin Joseph
Republican
b. Duluth, Minn., May 14, 1898
d. Bethesda, Md., April 14, 1964
U. S. Representative, 1927-33, 1935-45

MACDONALD, John Lewis
Democrat
b. Glasgow, Scotland, February 22, 1838
d. Kansas City, Mo., July 13, 1903

U. S. Representative, 1887-89

MACGREGOR, Clark
Republican
b. Minneapolis, Minn., July 12, 1922
U. S. Representative, 1961-71

MACKINNAN, George Edward
Republican
b. St. Paul, Minn., April 22, 1906
U. S. Representative, 1947-49

MANAHAN, James
Republican
b. near Chatfield, Minn., March 12, 1866
d. St. Paul, Minn., January 8, 1932
U. S. Representative, 1913-15

MARSHALL, Fred
Denocrat
b. Union Grove Township, near Grove City, Minn., March 13, 1906
U. S. Representative, 1949-63

MARSHALL, William R.
Republican
b. Boone County, Mo., October 17, 1825
d. Pasadena, Calif., January 8, 1876
Governor of Minnesota, 1866-70

MCCARTHY, Eugene Joseph
Democrat
b. Watkins, Minn., March 29, 1916
U. S. Representative, 1949-59
U. S. Senator, 1959-71

MCCLEARY, James Thompson
Republican
b. Ingersoll, Ontario, Canada, February 5, 1853
d. LaCrosse, Wis., December 17, 1924
U. S. Representative, 1893-1907

MCGILL, A. R.
Republican
b. Saegerstown, Pa., February 19, 1840
d. St. Paul, Minn., 1905
Governor of Minnesota, 1887-89

MERRIAM, William R.
b. Wadham's Mills, N. Y., July, 1849
d. February 18, 1931
Governor of Minnesota, 1889-93

MILLER, Clarence Benjamin
Republican
b. Pine Island, Minn., March 13, 1872
d. St. Paul, Minn., January 10, 1922
U. S. Representative, 1909-19

MONDALE, Walter F.
Democrat-Farmer-Labor
b. Ceylon, Minn., January 5, 1928
U. S. Representative, 1963-64
U. S. Senator, 1964-77
Vice President of the United States, 1977-

MORRIS, Robert Page Walter
Republican
b. Lynchburg, Va., June 30, 1853
d. Rochester, Minn., December 16, 1924
U. S. Representative, 1897-1903

NELSEN, Ancher
Republican
b. Renville County, near Buffalo Lake, Minn., October 11, 1904
U. S. Representative, 1959-

NELSON, Arthur Emanuel
Republican
b. Browns Valle, Minn., May 10, 1892
d. Chicago, Ill., April 11, 1955
U. S. Senator, 1942-43

NELSON, Knute
Republican
b. Voss, Norway, February 2, 1843
d. on train near Timonium, Md. en route to his home, April 28, 1923
U. S. Representative, 1883-89
Governor of Minnesota, 1893-95
U. S. Senator, 1895-1923

NEWTON, Walter Hughes
Republican
b. Minneapolis, Minn., October 10, 1880
d. Minneapolis, Minn., August 10, 1941
U. S. Representative, 1919-29

NOLAN, William Ignatius
Republican
b. St. Paul, Minn., May 14, 1874
d. Winona, Minn., August 3, 1943
U. S. Representative, 1929-33

NORTON, Daniel Sheldon
Union Conservative
b. Mount Vernon, Ohio
d. Washington, D. C., July 13, 1870
U. S. Senator, 1865-70

NYE, Frank Mellen
Republican
b. Shirley, Maine, March 7, 1852
d. Minneapolis, Minn., November 29, 1935
U. S. Representative, 1907-13

O'HARA, Joseph Patrick
Republican
b. Tipton, Iowa, January 23, 1895
U. S. Representative, 1951-59

OLSON, Alec Gerhard
Democrat
b. Mamre Township, Minn., September 11, 1930
U. S. Representative, 1963-67

OLSON, Floyd B.
Farmer-Laborite
b. Minneapolis, Minn., November 13, 1891
d. August 22, 1936
Governor of Minnesota, 1931-36

PETERSON, Hjalmar
Farmer-Laborite
Governor of Minnesota, 1936-37

PHELPS, William Wallace
Democrat
b. Oakland, Mich., June 1, 1826
d. Springlake, Mich., August 3, 1873
U. S. Representative, 1858-59

PILLSBURY, John Sargent
b. Sutton, N. H., July 29, 1828
d. 1901
Governor of Minnesota, 1876-82

PITTENGER, William
Republican
b. near Crawfordsville, Ind., December 29, 1885
d. Duluth, Minn., November 29, 1951
U. S. Representative, 1929-33, 1935-37, 1939-47

POEHLER, Henry
Democrat

b. Hiddeson, Lippe-Detmold, German, August 22, 1833
d. Henderson, Minn., July 18, 1912
U. S. Representative, 1879-81

PREUS, Jacob A. O.
Representative
b. Columbia County, Wis., August 28, 1883
d. May 24, 1961
Governor of Minnesota 1921-25

QUIE, Albert Harold
Republican
b. Wheeling Township, near Dennison, Minn., September 18, 1923
U. S. Representative, 1958-

RAMSEY, Alexander
Whig (Pennsylvania) Republican (Minnesota)
b. near Harrisburg, Pa., September 8, 1815
d. St. Paul, Minn., April 22, 1903
U. S. Representative, 1843-47 (Whig-Pennsylvania)
Governor of Territory of Minnesota, 1849-53
Governor of Minnesota, 1860-63
U. S. Senator, 1863-75 (Republican-Minnesota)
U. S. Secretary of War, 1879-81

RICE, Edmund
Democrat
b. Waitsfield, Vermont, February 14, 1819
d. White Bear Lake, Minn., July 11, 1889
U. S. Representative, 1887-89

RICE, Henry Mower
Democrat
b. Waitsfield, Vermont, November 29, 1817
d. San Antonio, Texas, January 15, 1894
U. S. Representative (Territorial Delegate), 1853-57
U. S. Senator, 1858-63

ROLVAAG, Karl F.
Democrat-Farmer-Labor
Governor of Minnesota, 1963-67

RYAN, Elmer James
Democrat
b. Rosemount, Minn., February 6, 1911
d. in automobile accident five miles north of Somerset, Wis., February 1, 1958

U. S. Representative, 1935-41

SABIN, Dwight May
Republican
b. near Marseilles, Ill., April 25, 1843
d. Chicago, Ill., December 22, 1902
U. S. Senator, 1883-89
Chairman, Republican National Committee, 1883-84

SCHALL, Thomas David
Republican
b. Reed County, Mich., June 4, 1878
d. in automobile accident, Washington, D. C., December 22, 1935
U. S. Representative, 1915-25
U. S. Senator, 1925-35

SELVIG, Conrad George
Republican
b. Rushford, Minn., October 11, 1877
d. Santa Monica, Calif., August 2, 1953
U. S. Representative, 1927-33

SHIELDS, James
Democrat (Illinois - Minnesota - Missouri)
b. Altmor, County Tyrone, Ireland, May 10, 1810
d. Ottumwa, Iowa, June 1, 1879
U. S. Senator, 1849, 1849-55 (Illinois), 1858-59 (Minnesota), 1879 (Missouri)

SHIPSTEAD, Henrik
Republican
b. Burbank, Minn., January 8, 1881
d. Alexandria, Minn., June 26, 1960
U. S. Senator, 1923-41 (Farmer-Laborite), 1941-47 (Republican)

SHOEMAKER, Francis Henry
Farmer-Laborite
b. in Flora Township, Minn., April 25, 1889
d. Minneapolis, Minn., July 24, 1958
U. S. Representative, 1933-35

SIBLEY, Henry Hastins
---- (Wisconsin - Minnesota)
b. Detroit, Mich., February 20, 1811
d. St. Paul, Minn., February 18, 1891
U. S. Representative (Territorial Delegate), 1848-49 (Wisconsin), 1849-53 (Minnesota)

Governor of Minnesota, 1858-60

SMITH, George Ross
Republican
b. St. Cloud, Minn., May 28, 1864
d. Minneapolis, Minn., November 7, 1952
U. S. Representative, 1913-17

SNIDER, Samuel Prather
Republican
b. Mount Gilead, Ohio, October 9, 1845
d. Minneapolis, Minn., September 24, 1928
U. S. Representative, 1889-91

STARKEY, Frank Thomas
Democrat
b. St. Paul, Minn., February 18, 1892
d. St. Paul, Minn., May 14, 1968
U. S. Representative, 1945-47

STASSEM Harold Edward
Republican
b. West St. Paul, Minn., April 13, 1907
Governor of Minnesota, 1938-45
Special Assistant to President Dwight D. Eisenhower with cabinet rank to direct studies of United States and world disarmament, 1955-58

STEARNS, Ozora Pierson
Republican
b. De Kalb, N. Y., January 15, 1831
d. Pacific Beach, Calif., June 2, 1896
U. S. Senator, 1871

STEENERSON, Halvor
Republican
b. Pleasant Springs, near Madison, Wis., June 30, 1852
d. Crookston, Minn., November 22, 1926
U. S. Representative, 1903-23

STEVENS, Frederick Clement
Republican
b. Boston, Mass., January 1, 1861
d. St. Paul, Minn., July 1, 1923
U. S. Representative, 1897-1915

STEWART, Jacob Henry
Republican
b. Clermont, N. Y., January 15, 1829
d. St. Paul, Minn., August 25, 1884
U. S. Representative, 1877-79

STRAIT, Horace Burton
Republican
b. Potter County, Pa., January 26, 1835
d. on a train at Juarez, Mexico en route to the United States, February 25, 1894
U. S. Representative, 1873-79, 1881-87

SWIFT, Henry A.
Republican
Governor of Minnesota, 1863-64

TAWNEY, James Albertus
Republican
b. Mount Pleasant Township, near Gettysburg, Pa., January 3, 1855
d. Excelsior Springs, Mo., June 12, 1919

TEIGAN, Henry George
Farmer-Laborite
b. Forest City, Iowa, August 7, 1881
d. Minneapolis, Minn., March 12, 1941
U. S. Representative, 1937-39

THYE, Edward John
Republican
b. near Frederick, S. Dak., April 26, 1896
d. Northfield, Minn., August 28, 1969
Governor of Minnesota, 1943-47
U. S. Senator, 1947-59

TOWNE, Charles Arnette
Democrat (Minnesota - New York)
b. near Pontiac, Mich., November 21, 1851
d. Tuscon, Ariz., October 22, 1958
U. S. Representative, 1895-97 (Republican-Minnesota)
U. S. Senator, 1900-01 (Democrat-Minnesota)
U. S. Representative, 1905-07 (Democrat-New York)

VANDYKE, Carl Chester
Democrat
b. Alexandria, Minn., February 18, 1881
d. Washington, D. C., May 20, 1919
U. S. Representative, 1915-19

VAN SANT, Samuel R.
Republican
b. Rock Island, Ill., May 11, 1844
d. October 3, 1936
Governor of Minnesota, 1901-05

VOLSTEAD, Andrew John
Republican
b. near Kenyon, Minn., October 31, 1860
d. Granite Falls, Minn., January 20, 1947
U. S. Representative, 1903-23

WAKEFIELD, James Beach
Republican
b. Winsted, Conn., March 21, 1825
d. Blue Earth, Minn., August 25, 1910
U. S. Representative, 1883-87

WASHBURN, William Drew
Republican
b. Livermore, Maine, January 14, 1831
d. Minneapolis, Minn., July 29, 1912
U. S. Representative, 1879-85
U. S. Senator, 1889-95

WEFALD, Knud
Farmer-Laborite
b. Kragero, Norway, November 3, 1869
d. St. Paul, Minn., October 25, 1936
U. S. Representative, 1923-27

WHITE, Milo
Republican
b. Fletcher, Vermont, August 17, 1830
d. Chatfield, Minn., May 18, 1913
U. S. Representative, 1883-87

WIER, Roy William
Democrat
b. Redfield, S. Dak., February 25, 1888
d. Seattle, Wash., June 27, 1963
U. S. Representative, 1949-61

WILKINSON, Morton Smith
Republican
b. Skaneateles, N. Y., January 22, 1819
d. Wells, Minn., February 4, 1894
U. S. Senator, 1859-65
U. S. Representative, 1869-71

WILSON, Eugene McLanahan
Democrat
b. Morgantown, Va. (now W. Va.), December 25, 1833
d. Nassau, New Providence Island, British West Indies, April 10, 1890
U. S. Representative, 1869-71

WILSON, Thomas
Democrat
b. Dungannon, County Tyrone, Ireland, May 16, 1827
d. St. Paul, Minn., April 3, 1910
U. S. Representative, 1887-89

WINDOM, William
Republican
b. Belmont County, Ohio, May 10, 1827
d. New York, N. Y., January 29, 1891
U. S. Representative, 1859-69
U. S. Senator, 1870-71, 1871-81
U. S. Secretary of the Treasury, 1881
U. S. Senator, 1881-83
U. S. Secretary of the Treasury, 1889-91

YOUNGDAHL, Luther W.
Republican
b. Minneapolis, Minn., May 29, 1896
Governor of Minnesota, 1947-51

YOUNGDAHL, Oscar Ferdinand
Republican
b. Minneapolis, Minn., October 13, 1893
d. Minneapolis, Minn., February 3, 1946
U. S. Representative, 1939-43

ZWACH, John M.
Republican
b. Gales Township, Minn., February 8, 1907
U. S. Representative, 1967-

PROMINENT PERSONALITIES

The following select list of prominent persons of Minnesota has been selected to indicate the valuable contributions they have made to American life.

BUTLER, Pierce
b. Dakota County, Minnesota, March 17, 1866
d. November 16, 1939
Associate Justice, U. S. Supreme Court, 1923-39

COFFMAN, Lotus Delta
b. Salem, Ind., January 7, 1875
d. September 22, 1938
Dean, College of Education, University of Minnesota, 1915-20
President, University of Minnesota, 1920-38
Author: Teacher Training Departments in Minnesota High School, 1920
The State University: Its Work and Problems, 1934

DONNELLY, Ignatius
b. Philadelphia, Pa., November 3, 1831
d. 1901
Member U. S. House of Representatives, 1863-69
Editor, Anti-Monopolist, 1874-79
Author: Atlantis, The Antediluvian World, 1882
The Great Cryptogram, 1888
Caesar's Column, 1891

FITZGERALD, F. Scott
(Francis Scott Key Fitzgerald)
b. St. Paul, Minn., September 24, 1896
d. December 21, 1940
Author: The Beautiful and the Damned, 1921
The Great Gatsby, 1925
Taps at Reveille, 1935
The Last Tycoon, 1941

FOLWELL, William Watts
b. Romulus, N. Y., February 14, 1833
d. September 18, 1929
Professor of Mathematics, Kenyon College, 1869
President, University of Minnesota, 1869-84
Professor, Political Science, University of Minnesota, 1875-1907
Author: Minnesota the North Star State
History of Minnesota, 4 vols.

HELLER, Walter Wolfgang
b. Buffalo, N. Y., August 27, 1915
Fiscal Economist, U. S. Treasury, 1942-46
Associate Professor of Economics, University of Minnesota, 1946-50
Professor of Economics, 1950-67
Economic Advisor to President John F. Kennedy
Regents Professor of Economics, University of Minnesota, 1967-

HILL, James Jerome
b. near Rockwood, Ontario, Canada, September 16, 1838
Mercantile businessman, 1856-65
Bought St. Paul and Pacific Railroad, with associates, 1878
Created Great Northern Railroad Company, (merger of all properties into one), 1890
President of Great Northern Railroad, 1882-1907
Chairman of the Board, Great Northern Railroad, 1907-12

JOHNSON, John Albert
b. St. Peter, Minn., July 28, 1861
d. 1909
Part owner, St. Peter Herald, became editor
Governor of Minnesota, 1905-09

KELLEY, Oliver Hudson
b. Boston, Mass., January 7, 1826
d. January 20, 1913
Clerk, U. S. Bureau of Agriculture, 1864-66
One of original organizers of National Grange of the Patrons of Husbandry, 1867
Secretary, National Grange of Patrons of Husbandry, 1867-78
Founder, Town Of Carrabelle, Florida, about 1876

MAYO, William J.
b. Le Sueur, Minn., June 29, 1861
d. July 28, 1939
Surgeon, known especially for operations for cancer and gallstones
Cofounder, with Brother Charles, of the Mayo Foundation for Medical Education and Research in affiliation with University of Minnesota which contributed $2,800,000 at Rochester, 1915

Received Gold Medal from American Medical Association, 1930

MERRITT, Leonidas
b. Chautauqua County, N. Y., February 20, 1844
d. Duluth, Minn., May 9, 1926
Discovered and located principal mines on Missabe Range, 1888-91
Constructed Duluth, Missabe and Northern Railway
Discovered and opened up copper and gold mines in west and in Mexico
Owner, Mountain Iron Bank
Member, Minnesota House of Representatives, 1893,94

NORSTAD, Lauris
b. Minneapolis, Minn., March 24, 1907
Supreme Allied Commander, Europe, SHAPE, 1956-63
President, Owens-Corning Fiberglas Corporation, 1964-67, chairman, 1967-72
Decorated: Distinguished Service Medal, Silver Star, Legion of Merit, Air Medal, Commander Legion of Honor

PILLSBURY, Charles Alfred
b. Warner, N. H., October 3, 1842
d. 1899
Founder, firm of Charles A. Pillsbury and Company, 1872, constructed largest mills in world
State Senator of Minnesota, 1877-87

PILLSBURY, John Sargent
b. Sutton, N. H., July 29, 1828
d. 1901

Founder, form of Charles A. Pillsbury and Company, 1872
Presented library building to East Minneapolis, 1900
Constructed and presented girls' home to the city of Minneapolis, 1901
State Senator of Minnesota, 1864-76
Governor of Minnesota, 1876-82

RICE, Henry Mower
b. Waitsfield, Vermont, November 29, 1817
d. San Antonio, Texas, January 15, 1894
Fur trader with Winnebago and Mississippi

Chippewa Indians
U. S. Senator, 1858-63

ROLVAAG, Ole Edvart
b. Norway, April 22, 1876
d. Northfield, Minn., November 5, 1931
Professor of Norwegian, St. Olaf College, Northfield, Minn., 1906-31
Author: Giants in the Earth, 1927

SWISSHELM, Jane Grey
b. Pittsburgh, Pa., December 6, 1815
d. Swissvale, Pa., July 22, 1884
Established Pittsburgh Saturday Visitor, weekly paper advocating abolition, temperance, woman's suffrage, 1847
Published St. Cloud Democrat, 1858-63

TALIAFERRO, Lawrence
b. Whitehall, Va., February 28, 1794
d. Bedford, Pa., January 22, 1871
Indian agent, Fort Snelling, Minn., in charge of Sioux and Chippewa Indians, 1819-27
In charge of Sioux Indians, 1827-39

VEBLEN, Thorstein Bunde
v. Cato, Wis., July 30, 1857
d. Palo Alto, Calif., August 3, 1929
Professor, University of Chicago, 1892-1906
Professor, University of Stanford, 1906-09
Professor of University of Missouri, 1911-18
Managing editor, Journal of Political Economy, 1896-1905
Author: The Theory of the Leisure Class, 1899
The Higher Learning in America, 1918
Absentee Ownership and Business Enterprise in Recent Times, 1923

VINCENT, George Edgar
b. Rockford, Ill., March 21, 1864
d. Greenwich, Conn., February 1, 1941
President, University of Minnesota, 1911-17
President, Rockefeller Foundation, 1917-29
Author: Social Mind and Education, 1896

FIRST STATE CONSTITUTION

CONSTITUTION OF MINNESOTA—1857.

We, the people of the State of Minnesota, grateful to God for our civil and religious liberty, and desiring to perpetuate its blessings, and secure the same to ourselves and our posterity, do ordain and establish this constitution.

ARTICLE I.

BILL OF RIGHTS.

SECTION 1. Government is instituted for the security, benefit, and protection of the people, in whom all political power is inherent, together with the right to alter, modify, or reform such government whenever the public good may require it.

SEC. 2. No member of this State shall be disfranchised, or deprived of any of the rights or privileges secured to any citizen thereof, unless by the law of the land, or the judgment of his peers. There shall be neither slavery nor involuntary servitude in the State, otherwise than in the punishment of crime, whereof the party shall have been duly convicted.

SEC. 3. The liberty of the press shall forever remain inviolate, and all persons may freely speak, write, and publish their sentiments on all subjects, being responsible for the abuse of such right.

SEC. 4. The right of trial by jury shall remain inviolate, and shall extend to all cases at law without regard to the amount in controversy, but a jury trial may be waived by the parties in all cases in the manner prescribed by law.

SEC. 5. Excessive bail shall not be required, nor shall excessive fines be imposed, nor shall cruel or unusual punishments be inflicted.

SEC. 6. In all criminal prosecutions, the accused shall enjoy the right to a speedy and public trial, by an impartial jury of the county or district wherein the crime shall have been committed, which county or district shall have been previously ascertained by law, and to be informed of the nature and cause of the accusation, to be confronted with the witnesses against him, to have compulsory process for obtaining witnesses in his favor, and to have the assistance of counsel in his defence.

SEC. 7. No person shall be held to answer for a criminal offence unless on the presentment or indictment of a grand jury, except in cases of impeachment, or in cases cognizable by justices of the peace, or arising in the army or navy, or in the militia, when in actual service in time of war or public danger, and no person for the same offence shall be put twice in jeopardy of punishment, nor shall he be compelled in any criminal case to [be] witness against himself, nor be deprived of life, liberty, or property without due process of law. All persons shall, before conviction, be bailable by sufficient sureties, except for capital offences, when the proof is evident or the presumption great; and the privileges of the writ of *habeas corpus* shall not be suspended, unless when, in cases of rebellion or invasion, the public safety may require.

SEC. 8. Every person is entitled to a certain remedy in the laws for all injuries or wrongs which he may receive in his person, property, or character; he ought to obtain justice freely, and without purchase; completely, and without denial; promptly and without delay, conformably to the laws.

SEC. 9. Treason against the State shall consist only in levying war against the same, or in adhering to its enemies, giving them aid and comfort. No person shall be convicted of treason unless on the testimony of two witnesses to the same overt act, or on confession in open court.

SEC. 10. The right of the people to be secure in their persons, houses, papers, and effects, against unreasonable searches and seizures, shall not be violated, and no warrant shall issue but upon probable cause, supported by oath or affirmation, and particularly describing the place to be searched, and the person or things to be seized.

SEC. 11. No bill of attainder, *ex post facto* law, nor any law impairing the obligation of contracts shall ever be passed, and no conviction shall work corruption of blood or forfeiture of estate.

SEC. 12. No person shall be imprisoned for debt in this State; but this shall not prevent the legislature from providing for imprisonment or holding to bail persons charged with fraud in contracting said debt. A reasonable amount of property shall be exempt from seizure or sale, for the payment of any debt or liability; the amount of such exemption shall be determined by law.

SEC. 13. Private property shall not be taken for public use without just compensation therefor, first paid or secured.

SEC. 14. The military shall be subordinate to the civil power, and no standing army shall be kept up in this State in time of peace.

SEC. 15. All the lands within this State are declared to be allodial, and feudal tenures of every description, with all their incidents, are prohibited. Leases and grants of agricultural land for a longer period than twenty-one years, hereafter made, in which shall be reserved any rent or service of any kind, shall be void.

SEC. 16. The enumeration of rights in this constitution shall not be construed to deny or impair others retained by and inherent in the people. The right of every man to worship God according to the dictates of his own conscience shall never be infringed, nor shall any man be compelled to attend, erect, or support any place of worship, or to maintain any religious or ecclesiastical ministry, against his consent, nor shall any control of, or interference with, the rights of conscience be permitted, or any preference be given by law to any religious establishment or mode of worship; but the liberty of conscience hereby secured shall not be so construed as to excuse acts of licentiousness, or justify practices inconsistent with the peace or safety of the State, nor shall any money be drawn from the treasury for the benefit of any religious societies, or religious or theological seminaries.

SEC. 17. No religious test or amount of property shall ever be required as a qualification for any office of public trust under the State. No religious test or amount of property shall ever be required as a qualification of any voter at any election in this State; nor shall any person be rendered incompetent to give evidence in any court of law or equity in consequence of his opinion upon the subject of religion.

ARTICLE II.

ON NAME AND BOUNDARIES.

SECTION 1. This State shall be called and known by the name of the State of Minnesota, and shall consist of and have jurisdiction over the territory embraced in the following boundaries, to wit: Beginning at the point in the centre of the main channel of the Red River of the North, where the boundary-line between the United States and the British possessions crosses the same; thence up the main channel of said river to that of the Bois des Sioux River; thence up the main channel of said river to Lake Traverse; thence up the centre of said lake to the southern extremity thereof; thence in a direct line to the head of Big Stone Lake; thence through its centre to its outlet; thence by a due-south line to the north line of the State of Iowa; thence east, along the northern boundary of said State, to the main channel of the Mississippi River; thence up the main channel of said river and following the boundary-line of the State of Wisconsin until the same intersects the Saint Louis River; thence down the said river to and through Lake Superior, on the boundary-line of Wisconsin and Michigan, until it intersects the dividing-line between the United States and British possessions; thence up Pigeon River and following said dividing-line to the place of beginning.

SEC. 2. The State of Minnesota shall have concurrent jurisdiction on the Mississippi and on all other rivers and waters bordering on the said State of Minnesota, so far as the same shall form a common boundary to said State, and any other State or States now or hereafter to be formed by the same; and said river and waters, and navigable waters leading into the same, shall be the common highways, and forever free, as well to the inhabitants of said State as to other citizens of the United States, without any tax, duty, impost, or toll therefor.

Sec. 3. The propositions contained in the act of Congress entitled "An act to authorize the people of the Territory of Minnesota to form a constitution and State government preparatory to their admission into the Union on an equal footing with the original States," are hereby accepted, ratified, and confirmed, and shall remain irrevocable without the consent of the United States; and it is hereby ordained that this State shall never interfere with the primary disposal of the soil within the same, by the United States, or with any regulations Congress may find necessary for securing the title to said soil to *bona-fide* purchasers thereof; and no tax shall be imposed on land belonging to the United States, and in no case shall non-resident proprietors be taxed higher than residents.

ARTICLE III.

DISTRIBUTION OF THE POWERS OF GOVERNMENT.

Section 1. The powers of government shall be divided into three distinct departments, the legislative, executive, and judicial; and no person or persons belonging to or constituting one of these departments shall exercise any of the powers properly belonging to either of the others, except in the instances expressly provided in this constitution.

ARTICLE IV.

LEGISLATIVE DEPARTMENT.

Section 1. The legislature of the State shall consist of a senate and house of representatives, who shall meet at the seat of government of the State, at such times as shall be prescribed by law.

Sec. 2. The number of members who compose the senate and house of representatives shall be prescribed by law, but the representation in the senate shall never exceed one member for every five thousand inhabitants, and in the house of representatives one member for every two thousand inhabitants. The representation in both houses shall be apportioned equally throughout the different sections of the State, in proportion to the population thereof, exclusive of Indians not taxable under the provisions of law.

Sec. 3. Each house shall be judge of the election, returns, and eligibility of its own members; a majority of each shall constitute a quorum to transact business, but a smaller number may adjourn from day to day, and compel the attendance of absent members, in such manner and under such penalties as it may provide.

Sec. 4. Each house may determine the rules of its proceedings, sit upon its own adjournment, punish its members for disorderly behavior, and, with the concurrence of two-thirds, expel a member, but no member shall be expelled a second time for the same offence.

Sec. 5. The house of representatives shall elect its presiding officer, and the senate and house of representatives shall elect such other officers as may be provided by law; they shall keep journals of their proceedings, and from time to time publish the same, and the yeas and nays, when taken on any question, shall be entered on such journals.

Sec. 6. Neither house shall, during a session of the legislature, adjourn for more than three days, (Sunday excepted,) nor to any other place than that in which the two houses shall be assembled, without the consent of the other house.

Sec. 7. The compensation of senators and representatives shall be three dollars per diem during the first session, but may afterwards be prescribed by law. But no increase of compensation shall be prescribed which shall take effect during the period for which the members of the existing house of representatives may have been elected.

Sec. 8. The members of each house shall in all cases, except treason, felony, and breach of the peace, be privileged from arrest during the session of their respective houses, and in going to or returning from the same. For any speech or debate in either house they shall not be questioned in any other place.

SEC. 9. No senator or representative shall, during the time for which he is elected, hold any office under the authority of the United States, or the State of Minnesota, except that of postmaster; and no senator or representative shall hold an office under the State, which had been created, or the emoluments of which had been increased, during the session of the legislature of which he was a member, until one year after the expiration of his term of office in the legislature.

SEC. 10. All bills for raising a revenue shall originate in the house of representatives, but the senate may propose and concur with amendments, as on other bills.

SEC. 11. Every bill which shall have passed the senate and house of representatives, in conformity to the rules of each house, and the joint rules of the two houses, shall, before it becomes a law, be presented to the governor of the State. If he approve, he shall sign and deposit it in the office of secretary of state for preservation, and notify the house where it originated of the fact. But if not, he shall return it, with his objections, to the house in which it shall have originated, when such objections shall be entered at large on the journal of the same, and the house shall proceed to reconsider the bill. If, after such reconsideration, two-thirds of that house shall agree to pass the bill, it shall be sent, together with the objections, to the other house, by which it shall likewise be reconsidered, and if it be approved by two-thirds of that house it shall become a law. But in all such cases the votes of both houses shall be determined by yeas and nays, and the names of the persons voting for or against the bill shall be entered on the journal of each house respectively. If any bill shall not be returned by the governor within three days (Sundays excepted) after it shall have been presented to him, the same shall be a law in like manner as if he had signed it, unless the legislature, by adjournment within that time, prevent its return, in which case it shall not be a law. The governor may approve, sign, and file in the office of the secretary of state, within three days after the adjournment of the legislature, any act passed during the three last days of the session, and the same shall become a law.

SEC. 12. No money shall be appropriated except by bill. Every order, resolution, or vote requiring the concurrence of the two houses (except such as relate to the business or adjournment of the same) shall be presented to the governor for his signature, and before the same shall take effect shall be approved by him, or being returned by him with his objections, shall be repassed by two-thirds of the members of the two houses, according to the rules and limitations prescribed in case of a bill.

SEC. 13. The style of all laws of this State shall be: "*Be it enacted by the legislature of the State of Minnesota.*" No law shall be passed unless voted for by a majority of all the members elected to each branch of the legislature, and the vote entered upon the journal of each house.

SEC. 14. The house of representatives shall have the sole power of impeachment, through a concurrence of a majority of all the members elected to seats therein. All impeachments shall be tried by the senate; and, when sitting for that purpose, the senators shall be upon oath or affirmation to do justice according to law and evidence. No person shall be convicted without the concurrence of two-thirds of the members present.

SEC. 15. The legislature shall have full power to exclude from the privilege of electing or being elected any person convicted of bribery, perjury, or any other infamous crime.

SEC. 16. Two or more members of either house shall have liberty to dissent and protest against any act or resolution which they may think injurious to the public or to any individual, and have the reason of their dissent entered on the journal.

SEC. 17. The governor shall issue writs of election to fill such vacancies as may occur in either house of the legislature. The legislature shall prescribe by law the manner in which evidence in cases of contested seats in either house shall be taken.

SEC. 18. Each house may punish by imprisonment, during its session, any person not a member who shall be guilty of any disorderly or contemptuous behavior in their presence, but no such imprisonment shall at any time exceed twenty-four hours.

SEC. 19. Each house shall be open to the public during the sessions thereof, except in such cases as in their opinion may require secrecy.

SEC. 20. Every bill shall be read on three different days in each separate house, unless in case of urgency two-thirds of the house where such bill is depending shall deem it expedient to dispense with this rule, and no bill shall be passed by either house until it shall have been previously read twice at length.

SEC. 21. Every bill having passed both houses shall be carefully enrolled, and shall be signed by the presiding officer of each house. Any presiding officer refusing to sign a bill which shall have previously passed both houses shall thereafter be incapable of holding a seat in either branch of the legislature, or hold any other office of honor or profit in the State, and in case of such refusal, each house shall, by rule, provide the manner in which such bill shall be properly certified for presentation to the governor.

SEC. 22. No bill shall be passed by either house of the legislature upon the day prescribed for the adjournment of the two houses. But this section shall not be so construed as to preclude the enrolment of a bill, or the signature and passage from one house to the other, or the reports thereon from committees, or its transmission to the executive for his signature.

SEC. 23. The legislature shall provide by law for an enumeration of the inhabitants of this State in the year one thousand eight hundred and sixty-five, and every tenth year thereafter. At their first session after each enumeration so made, and also at their first session after each enumeration made by the authority of the United States, the legislature shall have the power to prescribe the bounds of congressional, senatorial, and representative districts, and to apportion anew the senators and representatives among the several districts, according to the provisions of section second of this article.

SEC. 24. The senators shall also be chosen by single districts of convenient contiguous territory, at the same time that the members of the house of representatives are required to be chosen, and in the same manner, and no representative district shall be divided in the formation of a senate district. The senate districts shall be numbered in regular series, and the senators chosen by the districts designated by odd numbers shall go out of office at the expiration of the first year, and the senators chosen by the districts designated by even numbers shall go out of office at the expiration of the second year; and thereafter the senators shall be chosen for the term of two years, except there shall be an entire new election of all the senators at the election next succeeding each new apportionment provided for in this article.

SEC. 25. Senators and representatives shall be qualified voters of the State, and shall have resided one year in the State, and six months immediately preceding the election in the district from which they are elected.

SEC. 26. Members of the Senate of the United States from this State shall be elected by the two houses of the legislature in joint convention, at such times and in such manner as may be provided by law.

SEC. 27. No law shall embrace more than one subject, which shall be expressed in its title.

SEC. 28. Divorces shall not be granted by the legislature.

SEC. 29. All members and officers of both branches of the legislature shall, before entering upon the duties of their respective trusts, take and subscribe an oath or affirmation to support the Constitution of the United States, the constitution of the State of Minnesota, and faithfully and impartially to discharge the duties devolving upon him as such member or officer.

SEC. 30. In all elections to be made by the legislature, the members thereof shall vote *viva voce*, and their votes shall be entered on the journal.

SEC. 31. The legislature shall never authorize any lottery, or the sale of lottery-tickets.

ARTICLE V.

EXECUTIVE DEPARTMENT.

SECTION. 1. The executive department shall consist of a governor, lieutenant-governor, secretary of state, auditor, treasurer, and attorney-general, who shall be chosen by the electors of the State.

SEC. 2. The returns of every election for the officers named in the foregoing section shall be made to the secretary of state, and by him transmitted to the speaker of the house of representatives, who shall cause the same to be opened and canvassed before both houses of the legislature, and the result declared within three days after each house shall be organized.

SEC. 3. The term of office for the governor and lieutenant-governor shall be two years, and until their successors are chosen and qualified. Each shall have attained the age of twenty-five years, and shall have been a *bona-fide* resident of the State for one year next preceding his election. Both shall be citizens of the United States.

SEC. 4. The governor shall communicate by message to each session of the legislature such information touching the state and condition of the country as he may deem expedient. He shall be commander-in-chief of the military and naval forces, and may call out such forces to execute the laws, suppress insurrection, and repel invasion. He may require the opinion, in writing, of the principal officer in each of the executive departments, upon any subject relating to the duties of their respective offices; and he shall have power to grant reprieves and pardons, after conviction, for offences against the State, except in cases of impeachment. He shall have power, by and with the advice and consent of the senate, to appoint a State librarian and notary public; and such other officers as may be provided by law. He shall have power to appoint commissioners to take the acknowledgment of deeds, or other instruments in writing, to be used in the State. He shall have a negative upon all laws passed by the legislature, under such rules and limitations as are in this constitution prescribed. He may on extraordinary occasions convene both houses of the legislature. He shall take care that the laws be faithfully executed, fill any vacancy that may occur in the office of secretary of state, treasurer, auditor, attorney-general, and such other State and district offices as may be hereafter created by law, until the next annual election, and until their successors are chosen and qualified.

SEC. 5. The official term of the secretary of state, treasurer, and attorney-general shall be two years. The official term of the auditor shall be three years, and each shall continue in office until his successor shall have been elected and qualified. The governor's salary for the first term under this constitution shall be two thousand five hundred dollars per annum. The salary of the secretary of state for the first term shall be fifteen hundred dollars per annum. The auditor, treasurer, and attorney-general shall each, for the first term, receive a salary of one thousand dollars per annum. And the further duties and salaries of said executive officers shall each thereafter be prescribed by law.

SEC. 6. The lieutenant-governor shall be *ex-officio* president of the senate, and in case a vacancy should occur, from any cause whatever, in the office of governor, he shall be governor during such vacancy. The compensation of lieutenant-governor shall be double the compensation of a state senator. Before the close of each session of the senate they shall elect a president *pro tempore*, who shall be lieutenant-governor in case a vacancy should occur in that office.

SEC. 7. The term of each of the executive offices named in this article shall commence upon taking the oath of office after the State shall be admitted by Congress into the Union, and continue until the first Monday in January, 1860, except the auditor, who shall continue in office until the first Monday in January, 1861, and until their successors shall have been duly elected and qualified.

SEC. 8. Each officer created by this article shall, before entering upon his duties, take an oath or affirmation to support the Constitution of the United States and of this State, and faithfully discharge the duties of his office to the best of his judgment and ability.

SEC. 9. Laws shall be passed at the first session of the legislature after this State is admitted into the Union to carry out the provisions of this article.

ARTICLE VI.

JUDICIARY.

SECTION 1. The judicial power of the State shall be vested in a supreme court, district courts, courts of probate, justices of the peace, and such other courts, inferior to the supreme court, as the legislature may from time to time establish by a two-thirds vote.

SEC. 2. The supreme court shall consist of one chief justice and two associate justices, but the number of the associate justices may be increased to a number not exceeding four, by the legislature, by a two-thirds vote, when it shall be deemed necessary. It shall have original jurisdiction in such remedial cases as may be prescribed by law, and appellate jurisdiction in all cases, both in law and equity, but there shall be no trial by jury in said court. It shall hold one or more terms in each year, as the legislature may direct, at the seat of government, and the legislature may provide by a two-thirds vote that one term in each year shall be held in each or any judicial district. It shall be the duty of such court to appoint a reporter of its decisions. There shall be chosen by the qualified electors of the State one clerk of the supreme court, who shall hold his office for the term of three years, and until his successor is duly elected and qualified, and the judges of the supreme court, or a majority of them, shall have the power to fill any vacancy in the office of clerk of the supreme court until an election can be regularly had.

SEC. 3. The judges of the supreme court shall be elected by the electors of the State at large, and their term of office shall be seven years, and until their successors are elected and qualified.

SEC. 4. The State shall be divided by the legislature into six judicial districts, which shall be composed of contiguous territory, be bounded by county-lines, and contain a population as nearly equal as may be practicable. In each judicial district one judge shall be elected by the electors thereof, who shall constitute said court, and whose term of office shall be seven years. Every district judge shall, at the time of his election, be a resident of the district for which he shall be elected, and shall reside therein during his continuance in office.

SEC. 5. The district courts shall have original jurisdiction in all civil cases, both in law and equity, where the amount in controversy exceeds one hundred dollars, and in all criminal cases where the punishment shall exceed three months' imprisonment, or a fine of more than one hundred dollars, and shall have such appellate jurisdiction as may be prescribed by law. The legislature may provide by law that the judge of one district may discharge the duties of the judge of any other district not his own when convenience or the public interest may require it.

SEC. 6. The judges of the supreme and district courts shall be men learned in the law, and shall receive such compensation, at stated times, as may be prescribed by the legislature, which compensation shall not be diminished during their continuance in office, but they shall receive no other fee or reward for their services.

SEC. 7. There shall be established in each organized county in the State a probate court, which shall be a court of record, and be held at such times and places as may be prescribed by law. It shall be held by one judge, who shall be elected by the voters of the county for the term of two years. He shall be a resident of such county at the time of his election, and reside therein during his continuance in office, and his compensation shall be provided by law. He may appoint his own clerk, where none has been elected, but the legislature may authorize the election by the electors of any county of one clerk or register of probate for such county, whose powers, duties, term of office, and compensation shall be prescribed by law. A probate court shall have jurisdiction over the estates of deceased persons and persons under guardianship, but no other jurisdiction, except as prescribed by this constitution.

SEC. 8. The legislature shall provide for the election of a sufficient number of justices of the peace in each county, whose term of office shall be two years, and whose duties and compensation shall be prescribed by law: *Provided*, That no justice of the peace shall have jurisdiction of any civil cause where the amount in controversy shall exceed one hundred dollars, nor in a criminal cause where the punishment shall exceed three months' imprisonment or a fine of over one hundred dollars, nor in any cause involving the title to real estate.

SEC. 9. All judges other than those provided for in this constitution shall be elected by the electors of the judicial district, county, or city for which they shall be created, nor for a longer term than seven years.

SEC. 10. In case the office of any judge shall become vacant before the expiration of the regular term for which he was elected, the vacancy shall be filled by appointment by the governor, until a successor is elected and qualified. And such successor shall be elected at the first annual election that occurs more than thirty days after the vacancy shall have happened.

SEC. 11. The justices of the supreme court and the district courts shall hold no office under the United States, nor any other office under this State. And all votes for either of them for any elective office under this constitution, except a judicial office, given by the legislature or the people, during their continuance in office, shall be void.

SEC. 12. The legislature may at any time change the number of judicial districts or their boundaries, when it shall be deemed expedient, but no such change shall vacate the office of any judge.

SEC. 13. There shall be elected in each county where a district court shall be held one clerk of said court, whose qualifications, duties, and compensation shall be prescribed by law, and whose term of office shall be four years.

SEC. 14. Legal pleadings and proceedings in the courts of this State shall be under the direction of the legislature. The style of all process shall be "The State of Minnesota," and all indictments shall conclude "against the peace and dignity of the State of Minnesota."

SEC. 15. The legislature may provide for the election of one person in each organized county in this State, to be called a court commissioner, with judicial power and jurisdiction not exceeding the power and jurisdiction of a judge of the district court at chambers; or the legislature may, instead of such election, confer such powers and jurisdiction upon judges of probate in the State.

ARTICLE VII.

ELECTIVE FRANCHISE.

SECTION 1. Every male person of the age of twenty-one years or upwards, belonging to either of the following classes, who shall have resided in the United States one year, and in this State for four months, next preceding any election, shall be entitled to vote at such election, in the election district of which he shall at the time have been for ten days a resident, for all officers that now are, or hereafter may be, elective by the people:

First. White citizens of the United States.

Second. White persons of foreign birth, who shall have declared their intention to become citizens, conformably to the laws of the United States upon the subject of naturalization.*

Third. Persons of mixed white and Indian blood, who have adopted the customs and habits of civilization.

Fourth. Persons of Indian blood residing in this State, who have adopted the language, customs, and habits of civilization, after an examination before any district court of the State, in such manner as may be provided by law, and shall have been pronounced by said court capable of enjoying the rights of citizenship within the State.

SEC. 2. No person not belonging to one of the classes specified in the preceding section; no person who has been convicted of treason or any felony, unless restored to civil rights, and no person under guardianship, or who may be *non compos mentis* or insane, shall be entitled or permitted to vote at any election in this State.

SEC. 3. For the purpose of voting, no person shall be deemed to have lost a residence by reason of his absence while employed in the service of the United States; nor while engaged upon the waters of this State, or of the United States; nor while a student of any seminary of learning; nor while kept at any almshouse or asylum; nor while confined in any public prison.

SEC. 4. No soldier, seaman, or marine in the Army or Navy of the United States shall be deemed a resident of this State in consequence of being stationed within the same.

SEC. 5. During the day on which any election shall be held, no person shall be arrested by virtue of any civil process.

SEC. 6. All elections shall be by ballot, except for such town officers as may be directed by law to be otherwise chosen.

SEC. 7. Every person who, by the provisions of this article, shall be entitled to vote at any election, shall be eligible to any office which now is, or hereafter shall be, elective by the people in the district wherein he shall have resided thirty days previous to such election, except as otherwise provided in this constitution, or the Constitution and laws of the United States.

ARTICLE VIII.

SCHOOL-FUNDS, EDUCATION, AND SCIENCE.

SECTION 1. The stability of a republican form of government depending mainly upon the intelligence of the people, it shall be the duty of the legislature to establish a general and uniform system of public schools.

SEC. 2. The proceeds of such lands as are, or hereafter may be, granted by the United States for the use of schools within each township in this State, shall remain a perpetual school-fund to the State, and not more than one-third of said lands may be sold in two years, one-third in five years, and one-third in ten years; but the lands of the greatest valuation shall be sold first, provided that no portion of said lands shall be sold otherwise than at public sale. The principal of all funds arising from sales, or other disposition of lands, or other property, granted or intrusted to this State, in each township for educational purposes, shall forever be preserved inviolate and undiminished; and the income arising from the lease or sale of said school-lands shall be distributed to the different townships throughout the State, in proportion to the number of scholars in each township between the ages of five and twenty-one years, and shall be faithfully applied to the specific objects of the original grants or appropriations.

SEC. 3. The legislature shall make such provisions, by taxation or otherwise, as, with the income arising from the school-fund, will secure a thorough and efficient system of public schools in each township in the State.

SEC. 4. The location of the university of Minnesota, as established by existing laws, is hereby confirmed, and said institution is hereby declared to be the university of the State of Minnesota. All the rights, immunities, franchises, and endowments heretofore granted or conferred are hereby perpetuated unto the said university, and all lands which may be granted hereafter by Congress, or other donations, for said university purposes, shall vest in the institution referred to in this section.

ARTICLE IX.

FINANCES OF THE STATE, AND BANKS AND BANKING.

SECTION 1. All taxes to be raised in this State shall be as nearly equal as may be, and all property on which taxes are to be levied shall have a cash valuation, and be equalized and uniform throughout the State.

SEC. 2. The legislature shall provide for an annual tax, sufficient to defray the estimated expenses of the State for each year; and whenever it shall happen that such ordinary expenses of the State for any year shall exceed the income of the State for such year, the legislature shall provide for levying a tax for the ensuing year sufficient, with other sources of income, to pay the deficiency of the preceding year, together with the estimated expenses of such ensuing year.

SEC. 3. Laws shall be passed taxing all moneys, credits, investments in bonds, stocks, joint-stock companies, or otherwise, and also all real and personal property, according to its true value in money; but public burying-grounds, public school-houses, public hospitals, academies, colleges, universities, and all seminaries of learning, all churches, church property used for religious purposes, and houses of worship, institutions of purely public charity, public property used exclusively for any public purpose, and personal property to an amount not exceeding in value two hundred dollars for each individual, shall, by general laws, be exempt from taxation.

SEC. 4. Laws shall be passed for taxing the notes and bills discounted or purchased, moneys loaned, and all other property, effects, or dues of every description, of all banks, and of all bankers, so that all property employed in banking shall always be subject to a taxation equal to that imposed on the property of individuals.

SEC. 5. For the purpose of defraying extraordinary expenditures, the State may contract public debts, but such debts shall never in the aggregate exceed two hundred and fifty thousand dollars; every such debt shall be authorized by law for some single object to be distinctly specified therein; and no such law shall take effect until it shall have been passed by the vote of two-thirds of the members of each branch of the legislature, to be recorded by yeas and nays on the journals of each house respectively, and every such law shall levy a tax annually sufficient to pay the annual interest of such debt, and also a tax sufficient to pay the principal of such debt within ten years from the final passage of such law, and shall specially appropriate the proceeds of such taxes to the payment of such principal and interest, and such appropriation and taxes shall not be repealed, postponed, or diminished until the principal and interest of such debt shall have been wholly paid. The State shall never contract any debts for works of internal improvement, or be a party in carrying on such works, except in cases where grants of land or other property shall have been made to the State, especially dedicated by the grant to specific purposes, and in such cases the State shall devote thereto the avails of such grants, and may pledge or appropriate the revenues derived from such works in aid of their completion.

SEC. 6. All debts authorized by the preceding section shall be contracted by loan on State bonds of amounts not less than five hundred dollars each, on interest, payable within ten years after the final passage of the law authorizing such debt, and such bonds shall not be sold by the State under par. A correct registry of all such bonds shall be kept by the treasurer, in numerical order, so as always to exhibit the number and amount unpaid and to whom severally made payable.

SEC. 7. The State shall never contract any public debt, unless in time of war, to repel invasion or suppress insurrection, except in the cases and in the manner provided in the fifth and sixth sections of this article.

SEC. 8. The money arising from any loan made, or debt or liability contracted, shall be applied to the object specified in the act authorizing such debt or liability, or to the repayment of such debt or liability, and to no other purpose whatever.

SEC. 9. No money shall ever be paid out of the treasury of this State, except in pursuance of an appropriation by law.

SEC. 10. The credit of the State shall never be given or loaned in aid of any individual, association, or corporation.

SEC. 11. There shall be published by the treasurer, in at least one newspaper printed at the seat of government, during the first week of January in each year, and in the next volume of the acts of the legislature, detailed statements of all moneys drawn from the treasury during the preceding year, for what purposes, and to whom paid, and by what law authorized, and also of all moneys received, and by what authority, and from whom.

SEC. 12. Suitable laws shall be passed by the legislature for the safe-keeping, transfer, and disbursement of the State and school funds, and all officers and other persons charged with the same shall be required to give ample security for all moneys and funds of any kind, to keep an accurate entry of each sum received, and of each payment and transfer, and if any of said officers or other persons shall convert to his own use in any form, or shall loan with or without interest, contrary to law, or shall deposit in banks, or exchange for other funds, any portion of the funds of the State, every such act shall be adjudged to be an embezzlement of so much of the State funds as shall be thus taken, and shall be declared a felony, and any failure to pay over or produce the State or school funds intrusted to such persons, on demand, shall be held and taken to be *prima-facie* evidence of such embezzlement.

SEC. 13. The legislature may, by a two-thirds vote, pass a general banking law, with the following restrictions and requirements, viz:

First. The legislature shall have no power to pass any law sanctioning in any manner, directly or indirectly, the suspension of specie payments by any person, association, or corporation issuing bank-notes of any description.

Second. The legislature shall provide by law for the registry of all bills or notes issued or put in circulation as money, and shall require ample security in United States stock or State stocks for the redemption of the same in specie; and in case of a depreciation of said stocks, or any part thereof, to the amount of ten per cent. or more on the dollar, the bank or banks owning said stock shall be required to make up said deficiency by additional stocks.

Third. The stockholders in any corporation and joint association for banking purposes, issuing bank-notes, shall be individually liable in an amount equal to double the amount of stock owned by them for all the debts of such corporation or association, and such individual liability shall continue for one year after any transfer or sale of stock by any stockholder or stockholders.

Fourth. In case of the insolvency of any bank or banking association, the bill-holders thereof shall be entitled to preference in payment over all other creditors of such bank or association.

Fifth. Any general-banking law which may be passed in accordance with this article shall provide for recording the names of all stockholders in such corporations, the amount of stock held by each, the time of transfer, and to whom transferred.

ARTICLE X.

OF CORPORATIONS HAVING NO BANKING PRIVILEGES.

SECTION 1. The term "corporations," as used in this article, shall be construed to include all associations and joint-stock companies having any of the powers and privileges not possessed by individuals or partnerships, except such as embrace banking privileges; and all corporations shall have the right to sue and shall be liable to be sued in all courts, in like manner as natural persons.

SEC. 2. No corporation shall be formed under special acts, except for municipal purposes.

SEC. 3. Each stockholder in any corporation shall be liable to the amount of the stock held or owned by him.

SEC. 4. Lands may be taken for public way, for the purpose of granting to any corporation the franchise of way for public use. In all cases, however, a fair and equitable compensation shall be paid for such land and the damages arising from the taking of the same; but all corporations being common carriers, enjoying the right of way in pursuance to the provisions of this section, shall be bound to carry the mineral, agricultural, and other productions or manufactures on equal and reasonable terms.

ARTICLE XI.

COUNTIES AND TOWNSHIPS.

SECTION 1. The legislature may, from time to time, establish and organize new counties; but no new county shall contain less than four hundred square miles; nor shall any county be reduced below that amount; and all laws changing county-lines in counties already organized, or for removing county-seats, shall, before taking effect, be submitted to the electors of the county or counties to be affected thereby, at the next general election after the passage thereof, and be adopted by a majority of such electors. Counties now established may be enlarged, but not reduced below four hundred square miles.

SEC. 2. The legislature may organize any city into a separate county when it has attained a population of twenty thousand inhabitants, without reference to geographical extent, when a majority of the electors of the county in which such city may be situated, voting thereon, shall be in favor of a separate organization.

SEC. 3. Laws may be passed providing for the organization, for municipal and other town purposes, of any congressional or fractional townships in the several counties in the State: *Provided*, That when a township is divided by county lines, or does not contain one hundred inhabitants, it may be attached to one or more adjoining townships, or parts of townships, for the purposes aforesaid.

SEC. 4. Provision shall be made by law for the election of such county or township officers as may be necessary.

SEC. 5. Any county and township organization shall have such powers of local taxation as may be prescribed by law.

SEC. 6. No money shall be drawn from any county or township treasury except by authority of law.

ARTICLE XII.

OF THE MILITIA.

SECTION 1. It shall be the duty of the legislature to pass such laws for the organization, discipline, and service of the militia of the State as may be deemed necessary.

ARTICLE XIII.

IMPEACHMENT AND REMOVAL FROM OFFICE.

SECTION 1. The governor, secretary of state, treasurer, auditor, attorney-general, and the judges of the supreme and district courts may be impeached for corrupt conduct in office or for crimes and misdemeanors; but judgment in such case shall not extend further than to removal from office and disqualification to hold and enjoy any office of honor, trust, or profit in this State. The party convicted thereof shall, nevertheless, be liable and subject to indictment, trial, judgment, and punishment according to law.

SEC. 2. The legislature of this State may provide for the removal of inferior officers from office for malfeasance or nonfeasance in the performance of their duties.

SEC. 3. No officer shall exercise the duties of his office after he shall have been impeached and before his acquittal.

SEC. 4. On the trial of an impeachment against the governor, the lieutenant-governor shall not act as a member of the court.

SEC. 5. No person shall be tried on impeachment before he shall have been served with a copy thereof at least twenty days previous to the day set for trial.

ARTICLE XIV.

AMENDMENTS TO THE CONSTITUTION.

SECTION 1. Whenever a majority of both houses of the legislature shall deem it necessary to alter or amend this constitution, they may propose such alterations or amendments, which proposed amendments shall be published with the laws which have been passed at the same session, and said amendments shall be submitted to the people for their approval or rejection; and if it shall appear, in a manner to be provided by law, that a majority of voters present and voting shall have ratified such alterations or amendments, the same shall be valid to all intents and purposes, as a part of this constitution. If two or more alterations or amendments shall be submitted at the same time, it shall be so regulated that the voters shall vote for or against each separately.

SEC. 2. Whenever two-thirds of the members elected to each branch of the legislature shall think it necessary to call a convention to revise this constitution, they shall recommend to the electors to vote, at the next election, for members of the legislature, for or against a convention; and if a majority of all the electors voting at said election shall have voted for a convention, the legislature shall, at their next session, provide by law for calling the same. The convention shall consist of as many members as the house of representatives, who shall be chosen in the same manner, and shall meet within three months after their election for the purpose aforesaid.

ARTICLE XV.

MISCELLANEOUS SUBJECTS.

SECTION 1. The seat of government of the State shall be at the city of Saint Paul; but the legislature, at their first or any future session, may provide by law for a change of the seat of government by a vote of the people, or may locate the same upon the land granted by Congress for a seat of government to the State; and in the event of the seat of government being removed from the city of Saint Paul to any other place in the State, the capitol building and grounds shall be dedicated to an institution for the promotion of science, literature, and the arts, to be organized by the legislature of the State, and of which institution the Minnesota Historical Society shall always be a department.

SEC. 2. Persons residing on Indian lands within the State shall enjoy all the rights and privileges of citizens as though they lived in any other portion of the State, and shall be subject to taxation.

SEC. 3. The legislature shall provide for a uniform oath or affirmation to be administered at elections; and no person shall be compelled to take any other or different form of oath to entitle him to vote.

SEC. 4. There shall be a seal of the State, which shall be kept by the secretary of state, and be used by him officially, and shall be called by him the great seal of the State of Minnesota, and shall be attached to all official acts of the governor (his signature to acts and resolves of the legislature excepted) requiring authentication. The legislature shall provide for an appropriate device and motto for said seal.

SEC. 5. The territorial prison, as located under existing laws, shall, after the adoption of this constitution, be and remain one of the State prisons of the State of Minnesota.

SCHEDULE.

SECTION 1. That no inconvenience may arise by reason of a change from a territorial to a permanent State government, it is declared that all rights, actions, prosecutions, judgments, claims, and contracts, as well of individuals as of bodies-corporate, shall continue as if no change had taken place; and all process which may be issued under the authority of the Territory of Minnesota previous to its admission into the Union of the United States shall be as valid as if issued in the name of the State.

SEC. 2. All laws now in force in the Territory of Minnesota, not repugnant to this constitution, shall remain in force until they expire by their own limitation, or be altered or repealed by the legislature.

SEC. 3. All fines, penalties, or forfeitures accruing to the Territory of Minnesota shall inure to the State.

SEC. 4. All recognizances heretofore taken, or which may be taken before the change from a territorial to a permanent State government, shall remain valid, and shall pass to and may be prosecuted in the name of the State; and all bonds executed to the governor of the Territory, or to any other officer or court in his or their official capacity, shall pass to the governor or State authority, and their successors in office, for the uses therein respectively expressed, and may be sued for and recovered accordingly; and all the estate of property, real, personal, or mixed, and all judgments, bonds, specialties, choses in action, and claims and debts of whatsoever description, of the Territory of Minnesota, shall inure to and vest in the State of Minnesota, and may be sued for and recovered in the same manner and to the same extent by the State of Minnesota as the same could have been by the Territory of Minnesota. All criminal prosecutions and penal actions which may have arisen, or which may arise, before the change from a territorial to a State government, and which shall then be pending, shall be prosecuted to judgment and execution in the name of the State. All offences committed against the laws of the Territory of Minnesota before the change from a territorial to a State government, and which shall not be prosecuted before such change, may be prosecuted in the name and by the authority of the State of Minnesota, with like effect as though such change had not taken place; and all penalties incurred shall remain the same as if this constitution had not been adopted. All actions at law and suits in equity which may be pending in any of the courts of the Territory of Minnesota at the time of the change from a territorial to a State government may be continued and transferred to any court of the State which shall have jurisdiction of the subject-matter thereof.

SEC. 5. All territorial officers, civil and military, now holding their offices under the authority of the United States or of the Territory of Minnesota, shall continue to hold and exercise their respective offices until they shall be superseded by the authority of the State.

SEC. 6. The first session of the legislature of the State of Minnesota shall commence on the first Wednesday of December next, and shall be held at the capitol in the city of Saint Paul.

SEC. 7. The laws regulating the election and qualification of all district, county, and precinct officers shall continue and be in force until the legislature shall otherwise provide by law.

SEC. 8. The president of the convention shall, immediately after the adjournment thereof, cause this constitution to be deposited in the office of the governor of the Territory; and if after the submission of the same to a vote of the people, as hereinafter provided, it shall appear that it has been adopted by a vote of the people of the State, then the governor shall forward a certified copy of the same, together with an abstract of the votes polled for and against the said constitution, to the President of the United States, to be by him laid before the Congress of the United States.

SEC. 9. For the purposes of the first election, the State shall constitute one district, and shall elect three members to the House of Representatives of the United States.

SEC. 10. For the purposes of the first election for members of the State senate and the house of representatives, the State shall be divided into senatorial and representative districts, as follows, viz: First district, Washington County; second district, Ramsey County; third district, Dakota County; fourth district, so much of Hennepin County as lies west of the Mississippi; fifth district, Rice County; sixth district, Goodhue County; seventh district, Scott County; eighth district, Olmsted County; ninth district, Fillmore County; tenth district, Houston County; eleventh district, Winona County; twelfth district, Wabasha County; thirteenth district, Mower and Dodge Counties; fourteenth district, Freeborn and Faribault Counties; fifteenth district, Steele and Waseca Counties; sixteenth district, Blue Earth and Le Sueur Counties; seventeenth district, Nicollet and Brown Counties; eighteenth district, Sibley, Renville, and McLeod Counties; nineteenth district, Carver and Wright Counties; twentieth district, Benton, Stearns, and Meeker Counties; twenty-first district, Morrison, Crow Wing, and Mille Lac Counties; twenty-second district, Cass, Pembina, and Todd Counties; twenty-third district, so much of Hennepin County as lies east of the Mississippi; twenty-fourth district, Sherburne, Anoka, and Manomin Counties; twenty-fifth district, Chisago, Pine, and Isanti Counties; twenty-sixth district, Buchanan, Carlton, Saint Louis, Lake, and Itasca Counties.

SEC. 11. The counties of Brown, Stearns, Todd, Cass, Pembina, and Renville, as applied in the preceding section, shall not be deemed to include any territory west of the State line, but shall be deemed to include all counties and parts of counties east of said line as were created out of the territory of either at the last session of the legislature.

SEC. 12. The senators and representatives, at the first election, shall be apportioned among the several senatorial and representative districts as follows, to wit:

First district, two senators and three representatives.
Second district, three senators and six representatives.
Third district, two senators and five representatives.
Fourth district, two senators and four representatives.
Fifth district, two senators and three representatives.
Sixth district, one senator and four representatives.
Seventh district, one senator and three representatives.
Eighth district, two senators and four representatives.
Ninth district, two senators and six representatives.
Tenth district, two senators and three representatives.

Eleventh district, two senators and four representatives.
Twelfth district, one senator and three representatives.
Thirteenth district, two senators and three representatives.
Fourteenth district, one senator and three representatives.
Fifteenth district, one senator and four representatives.
Sixteenth district, one senator and three representatives.
Seventeenth district, one senator and three representatives.
Eighteenth district, one senator and three representatives.
Nineteenth district, one senator and three representatives.
Twentieth district, one senator and three representatives.
Twenty-first district, one senator and one representative.
Twenty-second district, one senator and one representative.
Twenty-third district, one senator and two representatives.
Twenty-fourth district, one senator and one representative.
Twenty-fifth district, one senator and one representative.
Twenty-sixth district, one senator and one representative.

SEC. 13. The returns from the twenty-second district shall be made to, and canvassed by, the judges of election at the precinct of Otter Tail City.

SEC. 14. Until the legislature shall otherwise provide, the State shall be divided into judicial districts as follows, viz:

The counties of Washington, Chisago, Manomin, Anoka, Isanti, Pine, Buchanan, Carlton, Saint Louis, and Lake, shall constitute the first judicial district.

The county of Ramsey shall constitute the second judicial district.

The counties of Houston, Winona, Fillmore, Olmsted, and Wabasha, shall constitute the third judicial district.

The counties of Hennepin, Carver, Wright, Meeker, Sherburne, Benton, Stearns, Morrison, Crow Wing, Mille Lac, Itasca, Pembina, Todd, and Cass, shall constitute the fourth judicial district.

The counties of Dakota, Goodhue, Scott, Rice, Steele, Waseca, Dodge, Mower, and Freeborn, shall constitute the fifth judicial district.

The counties of Le Sueur, Sibley, Nicollet, Blue Earth, Faribault, McLeod, Renville, Brown, and other counties in the State not included within the other districts, shall constitute the sixth judicial district.

SEC. 15. Each of the foregoing enumerated judicial districts may, at the first election, elect one prosecuting attorney for the district.

SEC. 16. Upon the second Tuesday, the 13th day of October, 1857, an election shall be held for members of the House of Representatives of the United States, governor, lieutenant-governor, supreme and district judges, members of the legislature, and all other officers designated in this constitution, and also for the submission of this constitution to the people, for their adoption or rejection.

SEC. 17. Upon the day so designated as aforesaid, every free white male inhabitant over the age of twenty-one years, who shall have resided within the limits of the State for ten days previous to the day of said election, may vote for all officers to be elected under this constitution at such election, and also for or against the adoption of this constitution.

SEC. 18. In voting for or against the adoption of this constitution, the words, "For constitution," or "Against constitution," may be written or printed on the ticket of each voter; but no voter shall vote for or against this constitution on a separate ballot from that cast by him for officers to be elected at said election under this constitution; and if upon the canvass of the votes so polled it shall appear that there was a greater number of votes polled for than against said constitution, then this constitution shall be deemed to be adopted as the constitution of the State of Minnesota; and all the provisions and obligations of this constitution, and of the schedule hereunto attached, shall thereafter be valid to all intents and purposes as the constitution of said State.

SEC. 19. At said election the polls shall be opened, the election held, returns made, and certificates issued in all respects as provided by law for opening, closing, and conducting elections and making returns of the same, except as hereinbefore specified, and excepting also that polls may be opened and elections held at any point or points, in any of the counties where precincts may be established as provided by law, ten days previous to the day of election, and not less than ten miles from the place of voting in any established precinct.

SEC. 20. It shall be the duty of the judges and clerks of election, in addition to the returns required by law for each precinct, to forward to the secretary of the Territory by mail, immediately after the close of the election, a certified copy of the poll-book, containing the name of each person who has voted in the precinct, and the number of votes polled for and against the adoption of this constitution.

SEC. 21. The returns of said election for and against this constitution, and for all State officers and members of the house of representatives of the United States, shall be made, and certificates issued, in the manner now prescribed by law for returning votes given for Delegate to Congress, and the returns for all district offices, judicial, legislative, or otherwise, shall be made to the register of deeds of the senior county in each district, in the manner prescribed by law, except as otherwise provided. The returns for all officers elected at large shall be canvassed by the governor of the Territory, assisted by Joseph R. Brown and Thomas J. Galbraith, at the time designated by law for canvassing the vote for Delegate to Congress.

SEC. 22. If, upon canvassing the votes for and against the adoption of this constitution, it shall appear that there has been polled a greater number of votes against than for it, then no certificates of election shall be issued for any State or district officer provided for in this constitution, and no State organization shall have validity within the limits of the Territory until otherwise provided for, and until a constitution for a State government shall have been adopted by the people.

H. H. SIBLEY,
President of Democratic Convention.

J. J. NOAH,
Secretary of Democratic Convention.

S. A. D. BALCOMBE,
President of Republican Convention.

L. A. BABCOCK,
Secretary of the Republican Convention.

SELECTED DOCUMENTS

The documents selected for this section have been chosen to reflect the interests or attitudes of the contemporary observer or writer. Documents relating specifically to the constitutional development of Minnesota will be found in volume five of Sources and Documents of United States Constitutions, a companion reference collection to the Columbia University volumes previously cited.

EARLY DAYS IN MINNESOTA

Harriet E. Bishop, one of the early settlers and residents of the state, describes her arrival, work and views of the developing state of Minnesota.

Source: Harriet E. Bishop. Floral Home; or, First Years of Minnesota. New York: Sheldon, Blakeman and Co., 1857.

WHY I CAME TO ST. PAUL.

THE question, why I came to St. Paul, will naturally arise in the mind of the reader. This cannot be better explained, nor with less appearance of egotism, than by the following letter from Rev. Dr. Williamson, of the Sioux Mission. It was addressed to the Board of National Popular Education, then in its embryo state, and by them placed in my hands.

"My present residence is on the utmost verge of civilization in the northwestern part of the United States, within a few miles of the principal village of white men in the territory that we suppose will bear the name of Minnesota, which some would render, 'clear water,' though strictly, it signifies slightly turbid or whitish water.

"The village referred to has grown up within a few years in a romatic situation on a high bluff of the Mississippi, and has been baptized by the Roman Catholics by the name of St. Paul. They have erected in it a small chapel, and constitute much the larger portion of the inhabitants. The Dakotas call it Im-mi-ja-ska (white rock), from the color of the sand-stone which forms the bluff on which the village stands. This village has five stores, as they call them, at all of which intoxicating drinks constitute a part, and I suppose the principal part, of what they sell. I would suppose the village contains a dozen or twenty families living near enough to send to school. Since I came to this neighborhood, I have had fre quent occasion to visit the village, and have been grieved to see so many children growing up entirely ignorant of God, and unable to read his Word, with no one to teach them. Unless your Society can send them a teacher, there seems to be little prospect of their having one for several years. A few days since I went to the place for the purpose of making inquiries in reference to the prospect of a school. I visited seven families, in which there were twenty-three children of proper age to attend school, and was told of five more, in which were thirteen more that it is supposed might attend, making thirty-six in twelve families. I suppose more than half of the parents of these children are unable to read themselves, and care but little about having their children taught. Possibly the priest might deter some from attending, who might otherwise be able and willing.

"I suppose a good female teacher can do more to promote the cause of education and true religion than a man. The natural politeness of the French (who constitute more than half the population) would cause them to be kind and courteous to a female, even though the priest should seek to cause opposition. I suppose she might have twelve or fifteen scholars to begin with, and if she should have a good talent for winning the affections of children (and one who has not should not come), after a few months she would have as many as she could attend to.

"One woman told me she had four children she wished to send to school, and that she would give boarding and a room in her house to a good female teacher, for the tuition of her children.

"A teacher for this place should love the Savior, and for his sake should be willing to forego, not only many of the religious privileges and elegances of New England towns, but some of the neatness also. She should be entirely free from prejudice on account of color, for among her scholars she might find not only English, French, and Swiss, but Sioux and Chippewas, with some claiming kindred with the African stock.

"A teacher coming should bring books with her sufficient to begin a school, as there is no book store within three hundred miles."

This was the first I had heard of St. Paul, or even of Minnesota, and the impression was at once riveted on my mind that *I must go;* and when, after two weeks of prayerful deliberation, the question was asked, "Who will go to St. Paul?" I could cheerfully, though tremblingly, respond, "*Here am I; send me.*" Every possible obstacle was presented; the difficulties of the almost unknown route; the condition of society; doubts as to a welcome by the people generally; the self-denials to be exercised; the privations to be endured—all of which were to me as so many incentives to persist in my decision. In short, I came because I was more needed here than at any other spot on earth, and because there was no other one of my class who felt it a duty to come.

Friends violently opposed. Those who dare not oppose did not encourage, and *vice versa.* It was evident that all considered it hazardous in the extreme, presuming on, yea, tempting Divine Providence. Only one had said, "*Go, and the Lord will be with you.*" And thus, with no human aid on which to rely, the arm of the Invisible was my support. And though comparatively ignorant of the world and its evils, I went forth to struggle with its waves; to tread the unknown future—a path hitherto unexplored—a thorny maze; but with the certainty that, where thorns abound, roses often bloom, and their sweet fragrance *has* refreshed me when weary, and been a sweet savor unto my soul.

I was happy then; I am happy in the retrospect. Never has a regret for the decision crossed my heart; on the contrary, it has ever been a theme of gratitude that I was enabled to overcome all impediments, and come at a time when no other one would venture.

REVIEW OF THE BOOK OF PROVIDENCE.

THE green hills of my dear native state had faded from my view; the dear dwellers at the old homestead were distanced, farther and yet farther, and for the first time I was without friend or kin, with more than two thousand miles to traverse to my final destination.

It is with no ordinary emotions that I review these pages in the book of Providence, where I was led "in a way I had not known." Surely, "goodness and mercy have followed me" since the morn I went forth at the bidding of my Master, to buffet alone the turbid billows of life.

Friends in Palmyra welcomed the strangers, and kindly entertained them on the Sabbath, and again "set them on their way rejoicing." This is the first incident of my journey to record. Never will that reception be forgotten, or cease to awaken grateful emotions. Some of that "eleven" have since been welcomed at the portals of glory!

Desirous to proceed, we knew of no good reason why we should not have passage on the Chesapeake, instead of waiting a day in Buffalo. But we failed in securing it. No reason was assigned, and we impatiently submitted. The fate of that steamer is well known; and friends still weep for the many who then found a grave in Lake Erie.

Unacquainted with the world, and unaccustomed to traveling alone, God prepared the hearts of Cleveland friends to attend me most of the long journey; and but for this I could scarce have accomplished it in safety. Then the facilities of western travel were very imperfect. There was not a railroad beyond Michigan, and staging over the worst of roads was the only mode of conveyance from Lake Michigan to the Mississippi. To obviate this difficulty, we journeyed by steam and stage to Cincinnati, where seventeen hundred miles of river course lay before us.

All spoke kindly of the object, though none approvingly; and many evidently regarded it as a wild chimera of the brain, and disappointment the inevitable result; and it was, indeed, generally believed, as I had been already assured, that I would never find a St. Paul. But there was never an instance when the sinking hope, or a desire to return, predominated in my breast.

Thus far an unseen hand had led me, and caused me most emphatically to feel that

> "'Tis Providence that shapes our ends,
> Rough-hew them as we will."

At St. Louis, the New York of the West, a combination of circumstances made me a passenger up the river in the same cabin with Mrs. Dr. Jones, of Galena, Illinois. Had there been the lurking of a doubt relative to the way, she was prepared to remove it. Having been twice at St. Paul, she was the first to define its locality. Her picture of it was not the most pleasing, but I had sought for a correct one and found it. Her words of cheer sent the sunshine of hope through my heart, and the meeting with her will ever be regarded as an important link in the chain of providences which marked my way. Time has proved her not a "summer friend," but a woman whose price is above rubies, whose worth and virtues shine with increasing lustre, a blessing to the world, and blessing all within the sphere of her influence. She kindly took the stranger in a strange land to her own home, put in her way the means of obtaining letters to the most important families in the vicinity, thus throwing light and cheerfulness on my, at best, uncertain path.

CHANGE OF SCENERY.

The time had come when "good bye" must be exchanged with the last of old and tried friends, the parting kiss exchanged with the last relative, to study new scenes and faces, and make new friends. Before turning homeward, they had commissioned the master of the steamer Lynx with my "safe landing" at the Mission of Dr. Williamson. Hope appeared in the distance—a halo of brightness encircling her form. Nature lent her charms to drive away the last lingerings of sadness, and to impart happiness before unequaled.

Hitherto, the character of the scenery had been pleasing, with little variety. Low banks sloped to the water's edge, and boundless prairies, chequered with fields of waving grain, and dotted with fine farm-houses, formed the landscape. Thriving villages and cities of a precocious growth skirted the river banks, while a degree of thrift and comfort I had little expected to see, met the view. The "wilderness and solitary place were made glad" by the fragrance of the rose, which bloomed in beauty amid the verdant thicket.

Galena, the great lead mart of northern Illinois and southern Wisconsin, is located on a river of the same name, seven miles from its entrance with the Mississippi. Here, the tame scenery merges at once into the picturesque and beautifully wild. Streets are cut through almost solid rock, and in some instances the roofs of three and four story blocks are on a level with the street above; everything indicating the indomitable energy and perseverance of the citizens.

Dubuque, in Iowa, twenty-five miles by the river windings above Galena, is surrounded by an irregular line of bluffs, bold and beautiful. This town, also rich in its mining interests, is one of the *fast* towns of the west.

The scenery now assumed a wild grandeur, varying with every view, and affording a literal feast for the eyes and heart. There was scarce an appearance of civilization for three hundred miles, if we except the old French town of Prairie du Chien, in Wisconsin, founded by some traders the same year that William Penn, under the shadow of his "broad brim," founded the city of "Brotherly Love." Here and there, upon the river bank, was a woodman's cabin, and again a claimant's, with a little patch of culinary vegetables in front, with, perhaps, a half-dozen half-clad children sporting about the door, who, on the ringing of the boat bell, would flee like frighted deer.

The Indian "hugged the shore" with his light canoe, or gazed with listless apathy from the bank, where he smoked his red-stone pipe.

"Slowly and surely" progressed the Lynx, and rapidly the hours sped on. All nature had conspired to form a glorious day when we first looked upon "Little Crow's Village," or Kaposia, where our boat headed on the morning of July 16th, 1847. The ringing of the bell occasioned a grand rush, and with telegraphic speed, every man, woman, and child flew to the landing.

To an unsophisticated eye like mine, the scene on shore was novel and grotesque, not to say repulsive; blankets and hair streaming in the wind; limbs uncovered; children nearly naked, the smaller ones entirely so, while a pappoose was ludicrously peeping over the shoulder of nearly every squaw. In the midst of the waiting throng appeared the Missionary and his sister.

A tear drop, which had suddenly formed in the heart, came welling up, but was arrested by a remark of the good humored Captain (peace to his memory), "That the Doctor was doing it up in fine style—he had got the whole village out for an escort!"

Before reaching the lower deck the crowd were thronging the plank and rushing upon the boat, arrayed in the most fantastic manner, and painted according to their fanciful notions of beauty.

I was received by the Missionaries with more than a kindly welcome, as presented by the Captain, with the playful injunction, "*Not to let the Indians scalp me!*" With other sage advice during this memorable up river trip, he had enjoined that *I should* "*kiss the pappooses,*" and *thereby secure the friendship of the band.* No sooner was I on shore than this *duty* became manifestly obvious—the greasy, smutty face of every mother's child being presented to afford me my initiatory lesson.

It was a moment of no ordinary interest—of calm, undefinable joy, when I entered the humble mission house. The "wild experiment" had become a reality; I stood upon ground which to me had before existed only in the ideal world.

Most of the principal Indians of the band, headed by the chief, followed me to the house, where a formal presentation took place, and I shook hands with each. They were curious to learn if I was a "big knife" (from the States), and why their expected annuities had not arrived, presuming that I must be conversant with all affairs at Washington. I had never felt so keenly the power of eye scrutiny.

Hitherto, mine had been a dreamy life, full of waking visions, with which reality was strangely blended. The shadowy vista of coming years had, from childhood, been crowded with rich imaginings. The Red Man in his far off home was, to my childish fancy, a being of the ideal world. Rarely had I seen a wandering remnant of the race, and I had formed no correct idea of him in his native state—on his own hunting grounds. Now I was on the very confines of civilization, surrounded by all the evidences of savage life. But soon the scene changed. Instead of stalwart men, half divested of clothing, with limbs naked and covered with grease and soot, to protect from mosquitos, there came a few native christian women for a prayer meeting. As I saw these untutored natives reverently bow, and heard their voices, in an unknown tongue, earnestly addressing a Throne of Grace, new but blissful emotions possessed my heart. Such pathos, such humility, such earnestness, I had rarely if ever witnessed. Yet they were few, very few, who found delight in these exercises. The majority of the Indians, still attached to their "wankons," though Gospel claims are urged upon them, choose the way "which goeth down to death."

Towards evening we strolled through their village, called at several "lodges," constructed of bark, and frolicked with the children in lieu of conversing with their mothers. At the lodge of the chief, a skin was placed without the door for my benefit, by his "superior," wife. This the mission lady urged me to accept, lest offence be given.

It is not an unimportant matter in frontier life to secure

the friendship of the natives. True they are ofttimes treacherous, and perhaps generally so, yet I am far from endorsing the belief that there are no exceptions. From the first they were kindly disposed toward me, regarding me with apparent interest, and many a time since have I been glad to welcome some of these my earliest Minnesota friends. The names of Old Betsey and Uncle John, of Harpa and Winona Zee, are familiar household words, and their good natured faces always brought a beam of merry sunshine into the house. And old Hocka-wash-ta was "always sure to be present when least wanted;" as the proverb runs of an evil genius, "no one could say where he was not."

Little Crow, the chief, whose calls were frequent, both at his village and after I had removed to St. Paul, is a tall, handsome man, with no striking expression of countenance. The youngest of seven brothers, all of whom have died by violent hands, ambitious for the chieftainship, attempted the life of his brother, wounding him severely, and he fearing the design would be eventually executed, ordered the younger to be shot. Thus the last but one of the name was gathered to his fathers. Little Crow possesses not the confidence of his band, who regard him as full of malice, intrigue and cunning. He often attended worship at the mission house and manifested some regard for the Scriptures, which he had learned to read.

FIRST SABBATH IN MINNESOTA.

THE day succeeding my arrival was the Sabbath, and as yet,

> "The sound of the church going bell,
> These prairies and bluffs never heard."

To the poor Indian all days are alike. Only a few had, who learned to keep it holy, assembled at the mission house for worship: a messenger being sent "to invite others to come in," the room was soon full. Some listened with profound attention; others remained in listless indifference, and others quietly dozed in their seats. A few were inclined to laugh, some left, but most remained until the services closed.

Then commenced their favorite game of ball, arrangements for the same having been going on all the morning, which continued for several successive days. The competitors for the prize placed their most valuable treasures upon a pole, which was carried around by two girls to receive the "stakes," and when the last was entered, the game commenced. The ball is thrown and caught by a small circle, with leather bands on one side, attached to a lever two or three feet long. When uncaught, the women fly off in its pursuit, and though they have no other interest in the game, they seem equally engaged with the men. In this game the wives of the Chief were most active. In passing our door one of them was kindly admonished of her sin, and reminded of the sorrow her Christian mother would have to know she was thus engaged. "She knew," she said, "her mother would feel very bad; but she was far away and could not know it, and besides, her boy's father (a term for husband) bade her '*so bad*,' she could not refuse." They literally "strip themselves for the race," and when fully aroused, ascend the bluff with the fleetness of a fawn—with unaffected grace of motion and dignity of mien.

Towards evening two Frenchmen were seen approaching the village. Suspicion was immediately rife with the villagers that they were bringing with them "fire water;" and some of them came in breathless haste, entreating Dr. Williamson to prevent it, for too well they knew its disastrous consequences. As a people, they were intemperate! Yet some had taken the pledge for a specified number of "moons," and did not wish the temptation there. But vicious and venal white men are responsible for the evil: forgetting that for this, "God will surely bring them into judgment."

In the afternoon, religious services in English were held—some half dozen persons coming from almost as many miles distant. And this was my first Sabbath—these were privileges I should rarely enjoy after a few more days! I thought of friends far, far away, worshipping God under *very* different circumstances; but I had no wish to return. I was happy in the rugged path I had chosen, for I felt, that now, life had commenced in earnest. Too long had it been spent in castle-building, with heart yearnings for *living purpose*.. True, the future was a blank book, and with what its pages might be filled, how could I divine? But I felt a calm, unwavering faith; a blessed consciousness that an unseen hand was leading me "in a way I had not known," and through "paths I had not seen before." Thus far the "Lord had directed my steps," and I knew that in Him I might still safely trust, and "move forward."

Nature was lavish with her charms, and the study which I had ever *so* much loved, became doubly interesting. I read the open page in a new light, under new impulses, for it was unmarred by the hand of Art. I seemed to look upon the world as it emanated from the hand of its Creator. Here was a solace for sadness; a substitute for society; a companion in solitude. A web of fibres had intertwined itself with my spiritual being, and a cup of nectar was the daily portion of my soul.

FIRST CANOE RIDE.

THE sun had never shone more brightly, nor the waters danced more gaily in its beams; never the birds sang more sweetly, nor a heart beat more in unison with the scene, than when, for the first time, I seated myself in a canoe, bound up stream, with two Indian girls at the "paddles." Probably my appearance was very ungraceful in their eyes, for they laughed merrily at my awkward sitting, and finally scolded, hinting at the probability of my getting a "ducking;" and there *was* sufficient proof that a well-balanced head was requisite for the safety of the light craft so heavily freighted.

Once under way, the novelty was pleasing in the extreme. The scenery was delightful, and amidst Nature's profound silence, scenes, tragic and comic, that had transpired in "these ends of the earth," were rehearsed by the accompanying missionaries. Soon the mosquitos began to show a "keen demand of appetite," and when, nearly frantic from their attacks, sea-sickness overpowered me, I yielded defenceless to their combined power.

The cry of "Patah-watah" arose from the squaws, and unbelief was changed to certainty by the peculiar notes of "high pressure in the distance," and the little "Argo" soon left us rocking in her wake. When we had passed up the "slough," and made our moorings beneath the bluff, where now stands the Upper Town, the first order of exercise was to place an Indian blanket beneath the shade of a maple, which was my first resting place in St. Paul. A cold crystal spring issued from a rock at a little distance, whence water was brought which had an almost magical effect, and I have always believed that none *so* pure ever came welling up to the surface from earth's centre.

The stranger, or the citizen even, would fail to recognize the scene which lay around and above, as any part of the ground now occupied by Minnesota's thriving capital. The high bluff almost forbade an attempted ascent. The noon-day breeze played joyfully among the huge maples and smaller trees, which effectually shut out the sun's gaze from the dancing brook, as it entered the Mississippi a few rods above. Following an Indian trail, we wound around the base of the bluff, when suddenly we were cheered by the sound of human voices, and stooping, could discern some women washing at the brook. The scene was enchanting. A vague and indefinite pleasure possessed the heart, and my only wish was that some appreciating friend might share the joys which Nature spread before me. How little was realized then, that here the "woodman's axe" was so soon to resound, the surveyor's chain to mark out a city, and the costly dwelling and substantial business block to rise, while numerous steamers should crowd the landing of that canoe, making our streets swarm with life, gayety and business bustle! Two years, and all this change is in progress; six more, and we have the actual reality, as if it were the work of magic. Workmen of every craft have been engaged, and the rapidity with which it is driven forward astonishes even themselves. Every department of business and science has its representatives; and the little fair-haired girl, with her meek blue eyes, who timidly stepped aside to let us pass, and remained half concealed by the bushes, looking more like a wood-nymph than the living personation of flesh and blood, has grown to be a scholar and a belle, as a part of this wonderful progress.

Turning from Nature, what a cheerless prospect greeted this view. A few log huts composed the "town"—three families the American population. With one of these, distant from the rest, a home was offered me. Their's was *the* dwelling—the only one of respectable size—containing three rooms and an attic.

The kindness and attention bestowed upon strangers in the early stages of western settlement, are proverbial the world over; nor are they overrated. A welcome hand, a warm heart, an open cabin, a full board, the best room and best bed—are sure to greet them. Every individual added to the population, adds an important item to its history. In after years, when it has swelled to thousands, hundreds may arrive in a day and remain unnoticed. Each one becomes absorbed in his own interest and is lost in the whirlpool of the rapid influx. Yet the heart beats as warmly as ever, and really bids the same welcome.

A few days previous to my coming, the "Red River train" arrived, an event at that time of semi-annual occurrence, and one hundred and twenty-one ox teams were encamped in the rear of the landing, where now stands the Lower Town. The principal men of the company had found fare and lodging with the few families, while the remainder encamped with their cattle, sleeping as they had done on the route, in their carts or upon the ground. Their cargoes, composed of valuable furs and rare specimens of Chippewa *embroidery*, were taken to St. Louis. These carts are without a particle of iron, but are very strong; before each a single ox is harnessed, and thus in

Indian file had they passed over nine hundred miles in fifty days. Of the Red River settlement we shall have more to say hereafter.

The captain of this caravan had brought with him his wife, a Scotch half-breed, for the first time out of their settlement, and a child of a year old, and a cow was attached to their cart for its benefit. All seemed full of health and life, with no apparent fatigue from the journey.

Such was the crowd in St. Paul, it was thought best that I should return to the Mission, to remain until it had dispersed, and proper arrangements could be made for the commencement of the school.

MINNESOTA IN 1859

This description presents much detailed information concerning the natural resources, various bodies of water, climate, industry and education of the state in the years prior to the Civil War. In addition a detailed picture of St. Paul and other locations is presented.

Source: The New World in 1859. Being the United States and Canada, Illustrated and Described. New York: C. E. Baillere, 1859. Part I.

MINNESOTA.

Minnesota, a territory of the United States, is bounded on the N. by British America, E. by Lake Superior and the State of Wisconsin, S. by Iowa and Missouri Territory, and W. by Missouri Territory. The Lake of the Woods, with a chain of small lakes and their outlets, form a part of the Northern boundary; the St. Croix and Mississippi a part of the eastern, and the Missouri and White Earth Rivers the western boundary. It lies between 42° 30′ and 49° N. lat., and between about 89° 30′ and 103° 30′ W. lon., being about 650 miles in extreme length from E. to W., and 430 from N. to S., including an area of nearly 166,000 square miles, or 106,240,000 acres.

Face of the Country.—Though there are no mountains in Minnesota, it is the most elevated tract of land between the Gulf of Mexico and Hudson's Bay, and from its central heights sends its waters to every point of the compass, but mostly to the N. and S. The position from which the Red River of the North and the St. Peter's take their opposite courses is almost exactly in the centre of the territory, and elevated about 2000 feet above the Gulf of Mexico. A plateau, called the "Coteau des Prairies," or "Prairie Heights," about 200 miles in length, and from 15 to 40 in breadth, runs through the middle of the southern part of Minnesota. Its greatest elevation is about 1916 feet above the level of the sea, and its average height about 1450 feet. The northern portion, which is the highest, is about 890 feet above Bigstone Lake, which lies in its vicinity. Passing the St. Peter's or Minnesota River, we come upon another range of heights, known as the "Coteau du Grand Bois," or the Wooded Heights, which extend for more than 100 miles nearly parallel with the "Coteau des Prairies." This ridge is mostly covered with an extensive forest of hard wood. Through the middle of the triangle which occupies the N. E. portion of the territory, runs a third range of heights, called the "Hauteurs de Terre," or "Highlands," which extend W. by S. about 300 miles, and form a dividing ridge, whence flow the waters that seek Lake Superior and the Mississippi in one direction, and Hudson's Bay in the other. A range of less altitude than the "Coteau des Prairies," but continuing in the same direction, forms the watershed of the streams flowing into the Missouri on the W., and those flowing into the Red River on the E. The rest of the country generally alternates between sandhills and swamps, and river bottoms and prairies. In the N., on the Red River, are extensive Savannas, level as a floor, while the central region and the portion between that and Lake Superior is much of it occupied with marshes, separated by hills of drift. West of the Coteau des Prairies, and Red River, the country has been but little explored; but that portion of it between the Rivière à Jacques and the Missouri is represented as composed of high rolling prairies.

Minerals.—The indications, from geological surveys of Minnesota, do not favour the hopes of great metallic wealth within its borders. Copper has been found, but in most instances it is not "in place," but appears to have been carried thither by the drift and boulders. The probability is that, of richer metallic ores than iron, this territory will not afford (except near Lake Superior) sufficient quantity to repay the labours of the miner; for if they exist at all, they probably lie at great depths. The indications are equally unfavourable to there being any large deposits of coal. A lead vein, 4 inches in thickness, was discovered on the Waraju River, by the geological corps of Professor Owen. The most remarkable mineral in this territory is the red pipestone, of which the Indians make their pipes, and which is believed to be peculiar to the region of the Coteau des Prairies. Salt is reported to exist in vast quantities between 47° and 49° N. lat., and 97° and 99° W. lon.

Lakes and Rivers.—Minnesota is, perhaps, even more deserving than Michigan of the appellation of the "Lake State," as it abounds in lacustrine waters of every size, from lakes of 40 miles in extent, to small ponds of less than a mile in circuit. These beautiful sheets of water give origin to rivers flowing N., S., and E.; some finding their way to the Atlantic through the mighty Mississippi and the Gulf of Mexico; others through the great lakes, Niagara, and the St. Lawrence; and others, again, pass off to the N., and seek the ocean through Hudson's Bay and Straits. The largest of these lakes, with the exception of Lake Superior, are the Lake of the Woods, Rainy Lake, Red, Minni-Wakan or Devil Lake, Leech, and Mille Lac, or Spirit Lake. These generally have clear, pebbly bottoms, and are well stocked with fish, among which are the white fish, pike, pickerel, maskelonge, sucker, perch and trout. Wild rice grows on the borders of many of them, especially at the North. Devil Lake, which is on the 48th parallel of N. lat., in the N. W. of Minnesota, is about 40 miles in length, by 15 in breadth, and its waters, which are brackish, have no visible outlet. Red Lake, on the same parallel, E. of Red River, with which it communicates, is divided into two portions, united by a strait of 2 miles in width, and covers about the same area as Devil Lake. Lake of the Woods, and Rainy Lake, (the former a large sheet of water, perhaps 100 miles in circuit,) are both on the N. E. boundary of the territory. Lake Pepin, a beautiful sheet of water, is a mere expansion of the Mississippi in the S. E. of this territory. The rivers and large streams of Minnesota are almost as numerous as its lakes. The far-famed Mississippi takes its humble origin from Itasca Lake, from whose pellucid waters it issues a rivulet of but a few feet in width, and first meandering in a N. E. direction through a number of small lakes, to receive their tribute, it turns to the S., and pursues its lordly way to its far distant exit in the Gulf of Mexico, laving in its course the shores of nine States and one territory. About 800 miles of its length are included within Minnesota, of which 500 are navigable, 200 below the Falls of St. Anthony, and 300 above. The Rum and St. Croix, tributaries of the Mississippi, drain the S. E. portion of the territory, and the Red River the northern, passing off into Hudson's Bay. It is the outlet of Traverse, Ottertail, Red, and several smaller lakes. It has a course of about 500 miles within Minnesota, though it does not flow directly north more than 200 miles in that distance. The Lake Superior slope is principally drained by the St. Louis and its branches, and by the outlets of that series of small lakes that form the N. E. boundary of Minnesota. The great valley formed by the slopes of the Coteau des Prairies and the Coteau du Bois is drained by the St. Peter's and its tributaries. This river runs first in a S. E., and then in a N. E. course, with a total length of from 400 to 500 miles, and is navigable for steamers, during high water, 56 miles above its mouth in the Mississippi, and 60 farther for keel-boats. Its principal branch is the Blue Earth or Mankota River. The St. Peter's, with the Crow Wing and Crow Rivers, are the principal tributaries of the Mississippi from the West. The Rivière à Jacques (reè ve-air' ah zhak) and the Sioux are the principal affluents of the Missouri from this territory. They both have an almost directly S. course, the former being about 600, and the latter 350 miles long. Nearly the whole western boundary is washed by the Missouri, which opens the western part of the territory to the commerce of the great Mississippi valley. The rivers of Minnesota abound in small falls and rapids, which, while they interrupt navigation, furnish extensive water-power.

Objects of Interest to Tourists.—If we except cataracts of the first magnitude and high mountains, Minnesota presents as great a variety of natural objects of interest as any portion of our widely extended domain.

Minnesota shares with Wisconsin in the falls and rapids of the St. Louis River, another picturesque and romantic display of nature's works. The rivers of Minnesota are filled with picturesque rapids and small falls, and often bordered with perpendicular bluffs of lime and sandstone, or gently sloping hills that gracefully recede from the water. This region is the paradise of the hunter: its prairies and forests are the home of many wild animals, and in its rivers and lakes swim great varieties of fish.

Climate.—The climate of this territory is severe, especially in the northern part. At the Pembina settlement, under the 49th parallel of latitude, the cold is frequently so great as to freeze quicksilver. Minnesota, in some parts, is too severe for Indian corn, but the dryness and steadiness of the cold favour wheat and other winter grains.

Soil and Productions.—The soil of Minnesota varies greatly. In the valleys of the rivers it is mostly excellent, especially in those of the St. Peter's, and of the Mississippi and its tributaries in the south-east of the territory. Above the Falls of St. Anthony, with the exception of the river alluvions and some prairie land, the country is generally covered with drift, interspersed with marshes, too wet for cultivation; but the elevated portion is often much of it of tolerable fertility, though inferior to the calcareous lands of the river bottoms, and not unfrequently covered with dwarf timber.

Forest Trees.—Parts of Minnesota are densely timbered with pine forests, and the ridges of the drift districts with small pine, birch, aspen, maple, ash, elm, hemlock, firs, poplar, and basswood. In the swamps between the ridges, the tamarack, cedar, and cypress are found; while the river bottoms furnish a good growth of oak, aspen, soft maple, basswood, ash, birch, white walnut, linden, and elm. Much of this timber on the poorer ridges, and in some of the marshes, is rather of a dwarf character. On the Rum, St. Croix, and Pine Rivers there are extensive forests of pine, of good, but not of the largest growth. According to Professor Owen, "a belt of forest crosses Minnesota in lat. 44° 30', which is remarkable for its unusual body of timber, in a country otherwise but scantily timbered." Taken as a whole, therefore, Minnesota can scarcely be called a well-wooded country. But here, as in other parts of the West, when the prairies are protected from fire, a growth of young timber soon springs up.

Animals.—Minnesota has always been a favourite hunting-ground of the Indians, and vast herds of buffalo, elk, deer, antelope, and other game still roam over the plains west of the Coteau des Prairies and the Red River. Deer, black bear, antelope, wolverine, otter, muskrat, mink, martin, wolf, and raccoon abound, and the moose and grizzly bear are occasionally met with. The prairies are frequented by grouse, pheasants, and partridges, and the streams by wild ducks and geese. The other birds are hawks, buzzards, harriers, owls, quails, plovers, larks, and a great variety of small birds. Among the water fowl are the pelican, tern, hooded sheldrake, bustard, broadbill, ruffle-headed duck, wood duck, teal, wild goose, and loon. Both the golden and bald eagle are occasionally met with. The rivers and lakes abound in fine fish, among which are the bass, cap, sunfish, pickerel, pike, catfish, whitefish, sucker, maskelonge, and trout.

Manufactures.—There are great capabilities in the innumerable rivers of Minnesota, with their falls and rapids, for manufacturing establishments. At present the conversion of her pine forests into boards, scantling, etc., constitutes the principal manufacture of this new and flourishing territory.

The best lands of Minnesota are on her two great navigable rivers, the Mississippi and St. Peter's; and the first acts of internal improvement needed by this territory will be the removal of some obstructions in these streams. It is among the probabilities that the great Pacific railway may traverse this region, as engineers are now examining the feasibilities of a northern route.

Commerce.—Minnesota has the advantage of two outlets for her productions; one by way of the Mississippi, to every portion of the Mississippi valley; and the other by way of Lake Superior, with the Lake States and with the East. The great export of this territory is her lumber.

Education.—Minnesota has a public system of free schools, which are under the general direction of a superintendent of common schools, and the local supervision of trustees. Every township containing not less than five families is considered a school district. "An act to incorporate the University of Minnesota," was passed February 25, 1851. This institution consists of five departments, namely, of science, literature, and art; of laws; of medicine; of agriculture; and of elementary instruction. Twelve regents, appointed by the legislature, manage its affairs. It is located at St. Anthony. The proceeds of all lands granted by the United States go to form a perpetual fund for the support of the university.

The information contained in the notice of the State of Wisconsin is copied from "Wisconsin as it is," by F. Gerhard, and that pertaining to the other States, from "Lippincott's Gazetteer. In a future edition the information will be brought down to a later period, in articles now preparing specially for this work.

ST. PAUL.

On our visit, St. Paul, like every other place, was affected with the prevailing epidemic, of "hard times," which had checked the ardour of some of her speculative citizens quite as much as it had done those of older cities. Consequently the town was dull, and also most of the people in it. All, however, with plenty of pluck, confident, that ere long, the little north-west city must of necessity go a-head again, and not stop till she is up sides with some of her south and easterly sister cities. Unlike most American towns, the streets of St. Paul are narrow, which we fancy will be regretted ere long. The streets, moreover, like those of New York, were dirty, and in bad order, but no doubt that in time will be rectified. The suburbs of St. Paul, however, are very beautiful, and many of the private residences, on the higher parts of the town, are very handsome and attractive. The population of St. Paul is variously estimated at from ten to fifteen thousand, of which a large proportion—probably a third—are foreigners; it contains a capitol and other public buildings, seven or eight churches, among which are two Episcopal, two Roman Catholic, two Presbyterian, and one or two Methodist and Baptist. The Romanists are also putting up a fine college, decidedly the handsomest public building in the place. The limestone, with which the whole town is underlaid, affords an admirable building stone, being very durable, handsome, and distributed in layers so as to be most conveniently worked.

There are three daily and three weekly papers published, which seem to have a large circulation, and to be ably conducted. There are also two German and a Norwegian paper, and one or two other small publications.

The principal street fronts the river for about two miles, and is lined with large stores of all kinds, to supply the increasing trade of that north-westerly region. The principal hotel is the Fuller House—a magnificent house, erected at a cost of $100,000, and fitted up with every modern comfort and convenience.

There are five railroads in this State, just commencing, or in course of completion: the Minnesota and Pacific—running from St. Paul to a point on the Missouri River; the North-western—from St. Paul to Lake Superior; the Cedar Valley and Minneapolis—from Minneapolis to Iowa line; the Transit and Root River—coming from Prairie du Chien; and the other from La Crosse, uniting at Rochester, and then continuing to St. Paul. These roads are all in progress, and Minnesota will soon have her network of railways, which will develope her resources, and give her a proud position among her sister States.

En passant, we may mention, that some of the merchants of St. Paul, who import their goods from Britain, do so direct from Liverpool via New Orleans, thence per steamer on the Mississippi. The saving is such, that the whole cost of transportation from Liverpool to St. Paul is very little more than the mere charges of transhipping *at New York*, and the freight *from there* to St. Paul. We have no doubt many importers on the other ports on the Mississippi and the Missouri will be following the example of the St. Paul merchants, the inland carriage from the Atlantic seaboard being extremely heavy on goods bound for the west and north-west provinces.

ST. PAUL TO ST. ANTHONY AND FALLS OF MINNEHAHA.

ENGAGING a horse and buggy at the Fuller House Hotel, we soon found ourselves en route for the falls, and a most delightful drive it is, over fine rolling uplands, covered with the precious staff of life, and waving and surging under the gentle breeze, ripening for the mower, and then to be sent abroad, perhaps thousands of miles, to feed the hungry in some of the cities in the east, or even Great Britain. On both sides of the road the landscape is beautiful, now and then showing glimpses of the Mississippi in the distance. At length we reached St. Anthony. Much as we have heard of the situation of St. Anthony, as the site for a manufacturing city, we did not expect to see so good a location for that purpose, and were, therefore, agreeably disappointed. The water-power is unlimited and inexhaustible—the great desideratum for a manufacturing city. The surrounding country is very fertile and the climate salubrious, in fact, similar to the more northerly portions of Canada West, with hot summers, tempered by the breezes from the west, with a very cold but dry atmosphere in winter.

At St. Anthony, the Mississippi has a perpendicular fall of 18 feet—the first which occurs in ascending the river.

The site of the village is on an elevated plain, and commands a fine view of the Falls, and is distant about 8 miles by land from St. Paul.

The University of Minnesota is established at St. Anthony, besides which, it contains 5 or 6 churches, about 30 stores, 2 newspaper offices, and several saw-mills, and other manufacturing establishments. The post-office is named St. Anthony's Falls. Population, about 2,500.

Opposite to the town of St. Anthony, is Minneapolis, on the opposite side of the river.

At night we stayed at St. Anthony. Next day we set out on a visit to Fort Snelling and Minnehaha. After crossing the suspension bridge, we soon found ourselves in Minneapolis, and at the celebrated Falls of Minnehaha—"the laughing water"—"the smile of the great spirit"—which will be found the prettiest little fall imaginable, complete in all its parts. A clear, sparkling stream comes rushing along the prairie, until it suddenly takes a leap of 60 feet over the precipice, and is lost in a deep dell, the sides of which are covered with shrubbery of luxurious growth. The rock over which the stream leaps, has been worn into an arch, and one can pass to and fro underneath, between the falls and the rock, with little or no inconvenience.

The recess behind the fall extends back nearly 50 feet, and, from that point, an extraordinary beautiful view of the fall is obtained, as the sun shines on the outside of it. The tourist can pass in at one side behind the fall, and find egress at the other side.

From the world-wide known Indian poem of Hiawatha, by Longfellow, we annex a few verses, descriptive of the scene now under notice:—

"Only once his pace he slackened,
Only once he paused or halted—
Paused to purchase heads of arrows
Of the ancient arrow-maker,
In the land of the Dacotahs,
Where the Falls of Minnehaha
Flash and gleam among the oak trees,
Laugh and leap into the valley.

"There the ancient arrow-maker
Makes his arrow-heads of sandstone,
Arrow-heads of chalcedony,
Arrow-heads of flint and jasper,
Smoothed and sharpened at the edges,
Hard and polished, keen and costly.

"With him dwelt his dark-eyed daughter,
Wayward as the Minnehaha,
With her moods of shade and sunshine;
Eyes that smiled and frowned alternate,
Feet as rapid as the river,
And as musical as laughter;
And he named her from the river,
From the waterfall he named her
Minnehaha, Laughing Water.

"Was it here for heads of arrows,
Arrow-heads of chalcedony,
Arrow-heads of flint and jasper,
That my Hiawatha halted
In the land of the Dacotahs?

"Was it not to see the maiden,
See the face of Laughing Water,
Peeping from behind the curtain;
Hear the rustling of her garments
From behind the waving curtain,
As we see the Minnehaha
Gleaming, glancing through the branches,
As one hears the Laughing Water
From behind its screen and branches?".

Altogether, it is a beautiful sight, in a most romantic spot, and should not be neglected by the tourist when at St. Paul. About 2 miles from the Falls, is situated Fort Snelling, sitting on the crest of a bold promontory, between the Mississippi and Minnesota Rivers. (See Fort Snelling.)

Before leaving St. Paul, the tourist will find a cave about 2 miles from the town, worthy of a visit. It is a subterranean curiosity in its way. Through it flows a stream of water, pure as crystal. The rock overhead is quite soft. To penetrate it, one or two guides are necessary with lights. Near the further end of it, there is said to be a small waterfall, and all in search of the wonderful underground should visit it to its utmost extremity. Starting from Milwaukee on Tuesday forenoon, we thus spent that night on board at Prairie du Chien, Wednesday night on board on Lake Pepin, and landed in St. Paul on Thursday morning at 9 o'clock. Saw all about St. Paul on Thursday; went to see the Falls and Fort Snelling on Friday, and returned to St. Paul on Saturday; Sunday, went to a neat little church there (Episcopal). On Monday afternoon, at 4 o'clock, we started on our return trip, accomplishing the distance from St. Paul to Prairie du Chien, 302 miles, in 17 hours, being fully 7 hours less time than we took to go up—the stream, of course, being against us on our upward trip.

LAKE SUPERIOR.

One of the trips now enjoyed by hundreds every year, from different parts of the United States and Canada, is that made by the splendidly appointed steamers which sail from Cleveland (Ohio) to the head of Lake Superior—touching at Detroit and Mackinaw. Passengers will also find steamers from Chicago for same points. The distance for the whole trip round is about 2000 miles. Time occupied about 8 days. Fare, $44 (£8 16s., stg.,) including the very best accommodation and meals.

In the summer season, it is one of the most delightful and invigorating trips which can be taken.

The commerce of the Lake Superior districts, as is well known, consists chiefly in copper and iron, from the mines situated in different parts.

The value of copper shipped in one year, from Ontonagon—the largest mining depot, and second town in size on the lake—exceeded $1,000,000 (£200,000, stg.).

From Marquette, it was expected that 200,000 tons of iron would be shipped last year. The other mining establishments are at the towns of Eagle River, Eagle Harbour, Copper Harbour, Bayfield, Lapoint, Bay City, Ashland, Grand Island City, Du Luth, etc., etc.

The City of Superior, situated on the Bay of Superior and Nemadji River, at the head of the lake, is the most important town. It was laid out in 1853. The population in January, 1857, was over 1,500—with 340 houses. In addition to being approached from Cleveland and Chicago, it is also reached from St. Paul, Minnesota, via the St. Croix and Brulé Rivers, per canoes.

With regard to the climate of the Lake Superior country, many erroneous impressions are entertained.

Professor David Dale Owen, the government geologist, in his report, says:—

"The health, even of the more marshy portions of this district, seems better than, from its appearance, one might expect. The long, bracing winters of these northern latitudes exclude many of the diseases which, under the prolonged heat of a southern climate, the miasm of the swamp engenders. At the Pembina settlement (in latitude 49°), owned by the Hudson's Bay Company, to a population of five thousand there was but a single physician, and he told me, that without an additional salary allowed him by the Company, the diseases of the settlement would not afford him a living."

Another writer says:—"None of the American lakes can compare with Lake Superior in healthfulness of climate during the summer months, and there is no place so well calculated to restore pressing miasms of the fever-breeding soil of the Southwestern States. This opinion is fast gaining ground among medical men, who are now recommending to their patients the healthful climate of this favoured lake, in preference to sending them to die in enervating southern latitudes.

"The waters of this vast inland sea, covering an area of over 32,000 miles, exercise a powerful influence in modifying the two extremes of heat and cold. The uniformity of temperature thus produced is highly favourable to animal and vegetable life. ***The most delicate fruits and plants are raised without injury,*** while four or five degrees further south they are destroyed by the early frosts."

Amongst the exports from there, we find "10 tons of Raspberry Jam," consigned to a party in Cleveland.

THE PICTURED ROCKS, LAKE SUPERIOR.

The subject of the sketch on the next page, is one of the most extraordinary natural curiosities which the region of the far north districts of America present.

The "Pictured Rocks" are situated on the eastern shore of Lake Superior at its outlet at St. Mary's River. The author of "Wisconsin as it is," in his description of Lake Superior, says:—

"But its greatest attraction is the 'Pictured Rocks,' which commence at this point and extend east about ten miles, and are so called from the various forms and colours presented by the rocks forming the shore of the lake. These rocks are of fine laminated sandstone, rising from 150 to 300 feet above the water level, and received the name of 'Pictured' from the brilliant colours formed from the oxides and sulphurets of metals, and vegetable fungi, which, by combination, form the most various pictures, and which, by the least imagination, assume the forms of ancient temples, religious processions, prairies, buffalo hunts, portraits, humorous scenes, until one is almost persuaded he is looking upon the magnificent masters, and not of nature. Among these, cataracts, falls and rivulets are pitching down in mighty volume, or dissipating their torrents into smoky mist."

MINNESOTA IN THE 1880'S

The following description by Charles Dudley Warner indicates the progress and development of the state as evidenced by conditions in the 1880's.

Source: Charles Dudley Warner. Studies in the South and West. New York: Harper & Brothers, 1889.

It is unnecessary to dwell upon the familiar facts that Minnesota is a great wheat State, and that it is intersected by railways that stimulate the enormous yield and market it with facility. The discovery that the State, especially the Red River Valley, and Dakota and the country beyond, were peculiarly adapted to the production of hard spring-wheat, which is the most desirable for flour, probably gave this vast region its first immense advantage. Minnesota, a prairie country, rolling, but with no important hills, well watered, well grassed, with a repellent reputation for severe winters, not well adapted to corn, nor friendly to most fruits, attracted nevertheless hardy and adventurous people, and proved specially inviting to the Scandinavians, who are tough and industrious. It would grow wheat without end. And wheat is the easiest crop to raise, and returns the greatest income for the least labor. In good seasons and with good prices it is a mine of wealth. But Minnesota had to learn that one industry does not suffice to make a State, and that wheat-raising alone is not only unreliable, but exhaustive. The grasshopper scourge was no doubt a blessing in disguise. It helped to turn the attention of farmers to cattle and sheep, and to more varied agriculture. I shall have more to say about this in connection with certain most interesting movements in Wisconsin.

The notion has prevailed that the North-west was being absorbed by owners of immense tracts of land, great capitalists who by the aid of machinery were monopolizing the production of wheat, and crowding out small farmers. There are still vast wheat farms under one control, but I am happy to believe that the danger of this great land monopoly has reached its height, and the tendency is the other way. Small farms are on the increase, practising a more varied agriculture. The reason is this: A plantation of 5000 or 15,000 acres, with a good season, freedom from blight and insects, will enrich the owner if prices are good; but one poor crop, with low prices, will bankrupt him. Whereas the small farmer can get a living under the most adverse circumstances, and taking one year with another, accumulate something, especially if he varies his products and feeds them to stock, thus returning the richness of his farm to itself. The skinning of the land by sending away its substance in hard wheat is an improvidence of natural resources, which belongs, like cattle-ranging, to a half-civilized era, and like cattle-ranging has probably seen its best days. One incident illustrates what can be done. Mr. James J. Hill, the president of the Manitoba railway system, an importer and breeder of fine cattle on his Minnesota country place, recently gave and loaned a number of blooded bulls to farmers over a wide area in Minnesota and Dakota. The result of this benefaction has been surprising in adding to the wealth of those regions and the prosperity of the farmers. It is the beginning of a varied farming and of cattle production, which will be of incalculable benefit to the North-west.

It is in the memory of men still in active life when the Territory of Minnesota was supposed to be beyond the pale of desirable settlement. The State, except in the north-east portion, is now well settled, and well sprinkled with thriving villages and cities. Of the latter, St. Paul and Minneapolis are still a wonder to themselves, as they are to the world. I knew that they were big cities, having each a population nearly approaching 175,000, but I was not prepared to find them so handsome and substantial, and exhibiting such vigor and activity of movement. One of the most impressive things to an Eastern man in both of them is their public spirit, and the harmony with which business men work together for anything which will build up and beautify the city. I believe that the ruling force in Minneapolis is of New England stock, while St. Paul has a larger proportion of New York people, with a mixture of Southern; and I have a fancy that there is a social shading that shows this distinction. It is worth noting, however, that the Southerner, transplanted to Minnesota or Montana, loses the *laisser faire* with which he is credited at home, and becomes as active and pushing as anybody. Both cities have a very large Scandinavian population. The laborers and the domestic servants are mostly Swedes. In forecasting what sort of a State Minnesota is to be, the Scandinavian is a largely determining force. It is a virile element. The traveller is impressed with the idea that the women whom he sees at the stations in the country and in the city streets are sturdy, ruddy, and better able to endure the protracted season of cold and the highly stimulating atmosphere than the American-born women, who tend to become nervous in these climatic conditions. The Swedes are thrifty, taking eagerly to politics, and as ready to profit by them as anybody; unreservedly American in intention, and on the whole, good citizens.

The physical difference of the two cities is mainly one of situation. Minneapolis spreads out on both sides of the Mississippi over a plain, from the gigantic flouring-mills and the canal and the Falls of St. Anthony as a centre (the falls being, by-the-way, planked over with a wooden apron to prevent the total wearing away of the shaly rock) to rolling land and beautiful building sites on moderate elevations. Nature has surrounded the city with a lovely country, diversified by lakes and forests, and enterprise has developed it into one of the most inviting of summer regions. Twelve miles west of it, Lake Minnetonka, naturally surpassingly lovely, has become, by an immense expenditure of money, perhaps the most attractive summer resort in the North-west. Each city has a hotel (the West in Minneapolis, the Ryan in St. Paul) which would be distinguished monuments of cost and elegance in any city in the world, and each city has blocks of business houses, shops, and offices of solidity and architectural beauty, and each has many private residences which are palaces in size, in solidity, and interior embellishment, but they are scattered over the city in Minneapolis, which can boast of no single street equal to Summit Avenue in St. Paul. The most conspicuous of the private houses is the stone mansion of Governor Washburn, pleasing in color, harmonious in design, but so gigantic that the visitor (who may have seen palaces abroad) expects to find a somewhat vacant interior. He is therefore surprised that the predominating note is homelikeness and comfort, and he does not see how a family of moderate size could well get along with less than the seventy rooms (most of them large) which they have at their disposal.

St. Paul has the advantage of picturesqueness of situation. The business part of the town lies on a spacious uneven elevation above the river, surrounded by a semicircle of bluffs averaging something like two hundred feet high. Up the sides of these the city climbs, beautifying every vantage-ground with handsome and stately residences. On the north the bluffs maintain their elevation in a splendid plateau, and over this dry and healthful plain the two cities advance to meet each other, and already meet in suburbs, colleges, and various public buildings. Summit Avenue curves along the line of the northern bluff, and then turns northward, two hundred feet broad, graded a distance of over two miles, and with a magnificent asphalt road-way for more than a mile. It is almost literally a street of palaces, for although wooden structures alternate with the varied and architecturally interesting mansions of stone and brick on both sides, each house is isolated, with a handsome lawn and ornamental trees, and the total effect is spacious and noble. This avenue commands an almost unequalled view of the sweep of bluffs round to the Indian Mounds, of the city, the winding river, and the town and heights of West St. Paul. It is not easy to recall a street and view anywhere finer than this, and this is only one of the streets on this plateau conspicuous for handsome houses. I see no reason why St. Paul should not become, within a few years, one of the notably most beautiful cities in the world. And it is now wonderfully well advanced in that direction. Of course the reader understands that both these rapidly growing cities are in the process of "making," and that means cutting and digging and slashing, torn-up streets, shabby structures alternating with gigantic and solid buildings, and the usual unsightliness of transition and growth.

Minneapolis has the State University, St. Paul the Capitol, an ordinary building of brick, which will not long, it is safe to say, suit the needs of the pride of the State. I do not set out to describe the city, the churches, big newspaper buildings, great wholesale and ware houses, handsome club-house (the Minnesota Club), stately City Hall, banks, Chamber of Commerce, and so on. I was impressed with the size of the buildings needed to house the great railway offices. Nothing can give one a livelier idea of the growth and grasp of Western business than one of these plain structures, five or six stories high, devoted to the several departments of one road or system of roads, crowded with busy officials and clerks, offices of the president, vice-president, assistant of the president, secretary, treasurer, engineer, general manager, general superintendent, general freight, general traffic, general passenger, perhaps a land officer, and so on—affairs as complicated and vast in organization and extensive in detail as those of a State government.

There are sixteen railways which run in Minnesota, having a total mileage of 5024 miles in the State. Those which have over two hundred miles of road in the State are the Chicago and North-western, Chicago, Milwaukee, and St. Paul, Chicago, St. Paul, Minneapolis, and Omaha, Minneapolis and St. Louis, Northern Pacific, St. Paul and Duluth, and the St. Paul, Minneapolis, and Manitoba. The names of these roads give little indication of their location, as the reader knows, for many of them run all over the North-west like spider-webs.

It goes without saying that the management of these great interests—imperial, almost continental in scope—requires brains, sobriety, integrity; and one is not surprised to find that the railways command and pay liberally for the highest talent and skill. It is not merely a matter of laying rails and running trains, but of developing the resources—one might almost say creating the industries — of vast territories. These are gigantic interests, concerning which there is such sharp rivalry and competition, and as a rule it is the generous, large-minded policy that wins. Somebody has said that the railway managers and magnates (I do not mean those who deal in railways for the sake of gambling) are the *élite* of Western life. I am not drawing distinctions of this sort, but I will say, and it might as well be said here and simply, that next to the impression I got of the powerful hand of the railways in the making of the West, was that of the high character, the moral stamina, the ability, the devotion to something outside themselves, of the railway men I met in the North-west. Specialists many of them are, and absorbed in special work, but I doubt if any other profession or occupation can show a proportionally larger number of broad-minded, fair-minded men, of higher integrity and less pettiness, or more inclined to the liberalizing culture in art and social life. Either dealing with large concerns has lifted up the men, or the large opportunities have attracted men of high talent and character; and I sincerely believe that we should have no occasion for anxiety if the average community did not go below the standard of railway morality and honorable dealing.

What is the *raison d'être* of these two phenomenal cities? why do they grow? why are they likely to continue to grow? I confess that this was an enigma to me until I had looked beyond to see what country was tributary to them, what a territory they have to supply. Of course, the railways, the flouring-mills, the vast wholesale dry goods and grocery houses speak for themselves. But I had thought of these cities as on the confines of civilization. They are, however, the two posts of the gate-way to an empire. In order to comprehend their future, I made some little trips north-east and north-west.

Duluth, though as yet with only about twenty-five to thirty thousand inhabitants, feels itself, by its position, a rival of the cities on the Mississippi. A few figures show the basis of this feeling. In 1880 the population was 3740; in 1886, 25,000. In 1880 the receipts of wheat were 1,347,679 bushels; in 1886, 22,425,730 bushels; in 1880 the shipments of wheat 1,453,647 bushels; in 1886, 17,981,965 bushels. In 1880 the shipments of flour were 551,800 bushels; in 1886, 1,500,000 bushels. In 1886 there were grain elevators with a capacity of 18,000,000 bushels. The tax valuation had increased from $669,012 in 1880 to $11,773,-729 in 1886. The following comparisons are made: The receipt of wheat in Chicago in 1885 was 19,266,-000 bushels; in Duluth, 14,880,000 bushels. The receipt of wheat in 1886 was at Duluth 22,425,730 bushels; at Minneapolis, 33,394,450; at Chicago, 15,982,524; at Milwaukee, 7,930,102. This shows that an increasing amount of the great volume of wheat raised in north Dakota and north-west Minnesota (that is, largely in the Red River Valley) is seeking market by way of Duluth and water transportation. In 1869 Minnesota raised about 18,000,000 bushels of wheat; in 1886, about 50,000,000. In 1869 Dakota grew no grain at all; in 1886 it produced about 50,000,000 bushels of wheat. To understand the amount of transportation the reader has only to look on the map and see the railway lines—the Northern Pacific, the Chicago, St. Paul, Minneapolis, and Omaha, the St.

Paul, Minneapolis, and Manitoba, and other lines, running to Duluth, and sending out spurs, like the roots of an elm-tree, into the wheat lands of the North-west.

Most of the route from St. Paul to Duluth is uninteresting; there is nothing picturesque except the Dalles of the St. Louis River, and a good deal of the country passed through seems agriculturally of no value. The approaches to Duluth, both from the Wisconsin and the Minnesota side, are rough and vexatious by reason of broken, low, hummocky, and swamp land. Duluth itself, with good harbor facilities, has only a strip of level ground for a street, and inadequate room for railway tracks and transfers. The town itself climbs up the hill, whence there is a good view of the lake and the Wisconsin shore, and a fair chance for both summer and winter breezes. The residence portion of the town, mainly small wooden houses, has many highly ornamental dwellings, and the long street below, following the shore, has many noble buildings of stone and brick, which would be a credit to any city. Grading and sewer-making render a large number of the streets impassable, and add to the signs of push, growth, and business excitement.

For the purposes of trade, Duluth, and the towns of Superior and West Superior, in Wisconsin, may be considered one port; and while Duluth may continue to be the money and business centre, the expansion for railway terminal facilities, elevators, and manufactures is likely to be in the Wisconsin towns on the south side of the harbor. From the Great Northern Elevator in West Superior the view of the other elevators, of the immense dock room, of the harbor and lake, of a net-work of miles and miles of terminal tracks of the various roads, gives one an idea of gigantic commerce ; and the long freight trains laden with wheat, glutting all the roads and sidings approaching Duluth, speak of the bursting abundance of the tributary country. This Great Northern Elevator, belonging to the Manitoba system, is the largest in the world ; its dimensions are 360 feet long, 95 in width, 115 in height, with a capacity of 1,800,000 bushels, and with facilities for handling 40 car-loads an hour, or 400 cars in a day of 10 hours. As I am merely illustrating the amount of the present great staple of the North-west, I say nothing here of the mineral, stone, and lumber business of this region. Duluth has a cool, salubrious summer and a snug winter climate. I ought to add that the enterprising inhabitants attend to education as well as the elevation of grain ; the city has eight commodious school buildings.

To return to the Mississippi. To understand what feeds Minneapolis and St. Paul, and what country their great wholesale houses supply, one must take the rail and penetrate the vast North-west. The famous Park or Lake district, between St. Cloud (75 miles north-west of St. Paul) and Fergus Falls, is too well known to need description. A rolling prairie, with hundreds of small lakes, tree fringed, it is a region of surpassing loveliness, and already dotted, as at Alexandria, with summer resorts. The whole region, up as far as Moorhead (240 miles from St. Paul), on the Red River, opposite Fargo, Dakota, is well settled, and full of prosperous towns. At Fargo, crossing the Northern Pacific, we ran parallel with the Red River, through a line of bursting elevators and wheat farms, down to Grand Forks, where we turned westward, and passed out of the Red River Valley, rising to the plateau at Larimore, some three hundred feet above it.

The Red River, a narrow but deep and navigable stream, has from its source to Lake Winnipeg a tortuous course of about 600 miles, while the valley itself is about 285 miles long, of which 180 miles is in the United States. This valley, which has astonished the world by its wheat production, is about 160 miles in breadth, and level as a floor, except that it has a northward slope of, I believe, about five feet to the mile. The river forms the boundary between Minnesota and Dakota; the width of valley on the Dakota side varies from 50 to 100 miles. The rich soil is from two to three feet deep, underlaid with clay. Fargo, the centre of this valley, is 940 feet above the sea. The climate is one of extremes between winter and summer, but of much constancy of cold or heat according to the season. Although it is undeniable that one does not feel the severe cold there as much as in more humid atmospheres, it cannot be doubted that the long continuance of extreme cold is trying to the system. And it may be said of all the North-west, including Minnesota, that while it is more favorable to the lungs than many regions where the thermometer has less sinking power, it is not free from catarrh (the curse of New England), nor from rheumatism. The climate seems to me specially stimulating, and I should say there is less excuse here for the use of stimulants (on account of "lowness" or lassitude) than in almost any other portion of the United States with which I am acquainted.

But whatever attractions or drawbacks this territory has as a place of residence, its grain and stock growing capacity is inexhaustible, and having seen it, we begin to comprehend the vigorous activity and growth of the twin cities. And yet this is the beginning of resources; there lies Dakota, with its 149,100 square miles (96,596,480 acres of land), larger than all the New England States and New York combined, and Montana beyond, together making a belt of hard spring-wheat land sufficient, one would think, to feed the world. When one travels over 1200 miles of it, doubt ceases.

I cannot better illustrate the resources and enterprise of the North-west than by speaking in some detail of the St. Paul, Minneapolis, and Manitoba Railway (known as the Manitoba system), and by telling briefly the story of one season's work, not because this system is bigger or more enterprising or of more importance in the West than some others I might name, but because it has lately pierced a comparatively unknown region, and opened to settlement a fertile empire.

The Manitoba system gridirons north Minnesota, runs to Duluth, puts two tracks down the Red River Valley (one on each side of the river) to the Canada line, sends out various spurs into Dakota, and operates a main line from Grand Forks westward through the whole of Dakota, and through Montana as far as the Great Falls of the Missouri, and thence through the cañon of the Missouri and the cañon of the Prickly-Pear to Helena—in all about 3000 miles of track. Its president is Mr. James J. Hill, a Canadian by birth, whose rapid career from that of a clerk on the St.

Paul levee to his present position of influence, opportunity, and wealth is a romance in itself, and whose character, integrity, tastes, and accomplishments, and domestic life, were it proper to speak of them, would satisfactorily answer many of the questions that are asked about the materialistic West.

The Manitoba line west had reached Minot, 530 miles from St. Paul, in 1886. I shall speak of its extension in 1887, which was intrusted to Mr. D. C. Shepard, a veteran engineer and railway builder of St. Paul, and his firm, Messrs. Shepard, Winston & Co. Credit should be given by name to the men who conducted this Napoleonic enterprise; for it required not only the advance of millions of money, but the foresight, energy, vigilance, and capacity that insure success in a distant military campaign.

It needs to be noted that the continuation of the St. Paul, Minneapolis, and Manitoba road from Great Falls to Helena, 98 miles, is called the Montana Central. The work to be accomplished in 1887 was to grade 500 miles of railroad to reach Great Falls, to put in the bridging and mechanical structures (by hauling all material brought up by rail ahead of the track by teams, so as not to delay the progress of the track) on 530 miles of continuous railway, and to lay and put in good running condition 643 miles of rails continuously and from one end only.

In the winter of 1886-87 the road was completed to a point five miles west of Minot, and work was done beyond which if consolidated would amount to about fifty miles of completed grading, and the mechanical structures were done for twenty miles west from Minot. On the Montana Central the grading and mechanical structures were made from Helena as a base, and completed before the track reached Great Falls. St. Paul, Minneapolis, and Duluth were the primary bases of operations, and generally speaking all materials, labor, fuel, and supplies originated at these three points; Minot was the secondary base, and here in the winter of 1886–87 large depots of supplies and materials for construction were formed.

Track-laying began April 2, 1887, but was greatly retarded by snow and ice in the completed cuts, and by the grading, which was heavy. The cuts were frozen more or less up to May 15th. The forwarding of grading forces to Minot began April 6th, but it was a labor of considerable magnitude to outfit them at Minot and get them forward to the work; so that it was as late as May 10th before the entire force was under employment.

The average force on the grading was 3300 teams and about 8000 men. Upon the track-laying, surfacing, piling, and timber-work there were 225 teams and about 650 men. The heaviest work was encountered on the eastern end, so that the track was close upon the grading up to the 10th of June. Some of the cuttings and embankments were heavy. After the 10th of June progress upon the grading was very rapid. From the mouth of Milk River to Great Falls (a distance of 200 miles) grading was done at an average rate of seven miles a day. Those who saw this army of men and teams stretching over the prairie and casting up this continental highway think they beheld one of the most striking achievements of civilization.

I may mention that the track is all cast up (even

where the grading is easy) to such a height as to relieve it of drifting snow; and to give some idea of the character of the work, it is noted that in preparing it there were moved 9,700,000 cubic yards of earth, 15,000 cubic yards of loose rock, and 17,500 cubic yards of solid rock, and that there were hauled ahead of the track and put in the work to such distance as would not obstruct the track-laying (in some instances 30 miles), 9,000,000 feet (board measure) of timber and 390,000 lineal feet of piling.

On the 5th of August the grading of the entire line to Great Falls was either finished or properly manned for its completion the first day of September, and on the 10th of August it became necessary to remove outfits to the east as they completed their work, and about 2500 teams and their quota of men were withdrawn between the 10th and 20th of August, and placed upon work elsewhere.

The record of track laid is as follows: April 2d to 30th, 30 miles; May, 82 miles; June, 70.8 miles; July, 100.6 miles; August, 115.4 miles; September, 102.4 miles; up to October 15th to Great Falls, 31.6 miles —a total to Great Falls of 545 miles. October 16th being Sunday, no track was laid. The track started from Great Falls Monday, October 17th, and reached Helena on Friday, November 18th, a distance of 98 miles, making a grand total of 643 miles, and an average rate for every working-day of three and one-quarter miles. It will thus be seen that laying a good road was a much more expeditious method of reaching the Great Falls of the Missouri than that adopted by Lewis and Clarke.

Some of the details of this construction and track-laying will interest railroad men. On the 16th of July 7 miles and 1040 feet of track were laid, and on the 8th of August 8 miles and 60 feet were laid, in each instance by daylight, and by the regular gang of track-layers, without any increase of their numbers whatever. The entire work was done by handling the iron on low iron cars, and depositing it on the track from the car at the front end. The method pursued was the same as when one mile of track is laid per day in the ordinary manner. The force of track-layers was maintained at the proper number for the ordinary daily work, and was never increased to obtain any special result. The result on the 11th of August was probably decreased by a quarter to a half mile by the breaking of an axle of an iron car while going to the front with its load at about 4 P.M. From six to eight iron cars were employed in doing this day's work. The number ordinarily used was four to five.

Sidings were graded at intervals of seven to eight miles, and spur tracks, laid on the natural surface, put in at convenient points, sixteen miles apart, for storage of materials and supplies at or near the front. As the work went on, the spur tracks in the rear were taken up. The construction train contained box cars two and three stories high, in which workmen were boarded and lodged. Supplies, as a rule, were taken by wagon-trains from the spur tracks near the front to their destination, an average distance of one hundred miles and an extreme one of two hundred miles. Steamboats were employed to a limited extent on the Missouri River in supplying such remote points as Fort Benton and the Coal Banks, but not more than fifteen per cent. of the transportation was done by steamers. A single item illustrating the magnitude of the supply transportation is that there were shipped to Minot and forwarded and consumed on the work 590,000 bushels of oats.

It is believed that the work of grading 500 miles of railroad in five months, and the transportation into the country of everything consumed, grass and water excepted, and of every rail, tie, bit of timber, pile, tool, machine, man, or team employed, and laying 643 miles of track in seven and a half months, from one end, far exceeds in magnitude and rapidity of execution any similar undertaking in this or any other country. It reflects also the greatest credit on the managers of the railway transportation (it is not invidious to mention the names of Mr. A. Manvel, general manager, and Mr. J. M. Egan, general superintendent, upon whom the working details devolved) when it is stated that the delays for material or supplies on the entire work did not retard it in the aggregate one hour. And every hour counted in this masterly campaign.

The Western people apparently think no more of throwing down a railroad, if they want to go anywhere, than a conservative Easterner does of taking an unaccustomed walk across country; and the railway constructors and managers are a little amused at the Eastern slowness and want of facility in construction and management. One hears that the East is antiquated, and does not know anything about railroad building. Shovels, carts, and wheelbarrows are of a past age; the big wheel-scraper does the business. It is a common remark that a contractor accustomed to Eastern work is not desired on a Western job.

On Friday afternoon, November 18th, the news was

flashed that the last rail was laid, and at 6 P.M. a special train was on the way from St. Paul with a double complement of engineers and train-men. For the first 500 miles there was more or less delay in avoiding the long and frequent freight trains, but after that not much except the necessary stops for cleaning the engine. Great Falls, about 1100 miles, was reached Sunday noon, in thirty-six hours, an average of over thirty miles an hour. A part of the time the speed was as much as fifty miles an hour. The track was solid, evenly graded, heavily tied, well aligned, and the cars ran over it with no more swing and bounce than on an old road. The only exception to this is the piece from Great Falls to Helena, which had not been surfaced all the way. It is excellent railway construction, and it is necessary to emphasize this when we consider the rapidity with which it was built.

The company has built this road without land grant or subsidy of any kind. The Montana extension, from Minot, Dakota, to Great Falls, runs mostly through Indian and military reservations, permission to pass through being given by special Act of Congress, and the company buying 200 feet road-way. Little of it, therefore, is open to settlement.

* * *

* * *

In St. Paul and Minneapolis one thing notable is the cordial hospitality, another is the public spirit, and another is the intense devotion to business, the forecast and alertness in new enterprises. Where society is fluid and on the move, it seems comparatively easy to interest the citizens in any scheme for the public good. The public spirit of those cities is admirable. One notices also an uncommon power of organization, of devices for saving time. An illustration of this is the immense railway transfer ground here. Midway between the cities is a mile square of land where all the great railway lines meet, and by means of communicating tracks easily and cheaply exchange freight cars, immensely increasing the facility and lessening the cost of transportation. Another illustration of system is the State office of Public Examiner, an office peculiar to Minnesota, an office supervising banks, public institutions, and county treasuries, by means of which a uniform system of accounting is enforced for all public funds, and safety is insured.

There is a large furniture and furnishing store in Minneapolis, well sustained by the public, which gives one a new idea of the taste of the North-west. A community that buys furniture so elegant and chaste in design, and stuffs and decorations so æsthetically good, as this shop offers it, is certainly not deficient either in material refinement or the means to gratify the love of it.

What is there besides this tremendous energy, very material prosperity, and undeniable refinement in living? I do not know that the excellently managed public-school system offers anything peculiar for comment. But the High-school in St. Paul is worth a visit. So far as I could judge, the method of teaching is admirable, and produces good results. It has no rules, nor any espionage. Scholars are put upon their honor. One object of education being character, it is well to have good behavior consist, not in conformity to artificial laws existing only in school, but to principles of good conduct that should prevail everywhere. There is system here, but the conduct expected is that of well-bred boys and girls anywhere. The plan works well, and there are very few cases of discipline. A manual training school is attached—a notion growing in favor in the West, and practised in a scientific and truly educational spirit. Attendance is not compulsory, but a considerable proportion of the pupils, boys and girls, spend a certain number of hours each week in the workshops, learning the use of tools, and making simple objects to an accurate scale from drawings on the blackboard. The design is not at all to teach a trade. The object is strictly educational, not simply to give manual facility and knowledge in the use of tools, but to teach accuracy, the mental training that there is in working out a definite, specific purpose.

The State University is still in a formative condition, and has attached to it a preparatory school. Its first class graduated only in 1872. It sends out on an average about twenty graduates a year in the various departments, science, literature, mechanic arts, and agriculture. The bane of a State university is politics, and in the West the hand of the Granger is on the college, endeavoring to make it "practical." Probably this modern idea of education will have to run its course, and so long as it is running its course the Eastern colleges which adhere to the idea of intellectual discipline will attract the young men who value a liberal rather than a material education. The State University of Minnesota is thriving in the enlargement of its facilities. About one-third of its scholars are women, but I notice that in the last catalogue, in the Senior Class of twenty-six there is only one woman. There are two independent institutions also that should be mentioned, both within the limits of St. Paul, the Hamline University, under Methodist auspices, and the McAllister College, under Presbyterian. I did not visit the former, but the latter, at least, though just beginning, has the idea of a classical education foremost, and does not adopt co-education. Its library is well begun by the gift of a miscellaneous collection, containing many rare and old books, by the Rev. E. D. Neill, the well-known antiquarian, who has done so much to illuminate the colonial history of Virginia and Maryland. In the State Historical Society, which has rooms in the Capitol in St. Paul, a vigorous and well-managed society, is a valuable collection of books illustrating the history of the North-west. The visitor will notice in St. Paul quite as much taste for reading among business men as exists elsewhere, a growing fancy for rare books, and find some private collections of interest. Though music and art cannot be said to be generally cultivated, there are in private circles musical enthusiasm and musical ability, and many of the best examples of modern painting are to be found in private houses. Indeed, there is one gallery in which is a collection of pictures by foreign artists that would be notable in any city. These things are mentioned as indications of a liberalizing use of wealth.

MINNESOTA FARM LIFE -- EARLY 20TH Century

The following is an interesting description of the lives, problems, needs, concerns and desires of the many farmers who resided on the Minnesota prairies during the first decade of the twentieth century. The methods of attracting workers, and their work and pay are also discussed.

Source: Clifton Johnson. Highways and Byways of the Mississippi Valley. New York: The Macmillan Company, 1906.

ON THE MINNESOTA PRAIRIES

I WAS at Dobbsdale, a country village in the southern part of the state. It was just after breakfast and I had sat down in the office of the town's one hotel with the intention of starting out for a ramble, presently. The room was rather dubiously odorous of more or less ancient tobacco fumes; but that is to be expected in the average hotel. The big stove was flanked on either side by a spittoon box — a shallow wooden affair with the bottom sprinkled with dirt, and the dirt sprinkled with burnt matches, cigar stubs, old quids, and other filth. The hotel was a clumsy two-story wooden building only separated from the street by a board walk. Several hitching posts bordered the walk and also a stout plank, which had been adjusted to serve for a seat when weather and inclination favored such use. There were board walks all through the village, though many pieces were shattered or missing. In the village centre was the usual straggling cluster of low stores, some of them brick, some wooden; but what was especially distinctive about the place was its abundance of trees. Every street was lined with them, and there were many others in yards and along boundaries. They were well grown, and made the town a kind of human bird's nest, with an aspect charmingly peaceful and shadowy.

The region had been settled within the memory of persons still living, and Mr. Dobbs, the ancestor of the town, was not only alive, but hale and hearty and good for many years yet. He was the town's chief citizen, just as he had been from the first. It seemed odd that he should have called the place Dobbs's *dale;* for there was no dale, and the country about was almost as level as it possibly could be. But I suppose dale appealed to his fancy. He evidently had a touch of poetry in his nature, as it was due to his hobby that the hamlet was so well wooded. He began planting trees when he first came, and had never ceased planting them since.

"The way I happened to settle in this country," said he, "ware that my father fit in the War of 1812, and he got a warrant from the government for a quarter section of land. So my brother and I come here in 1856 and brought a sawmill and got out timber and built us a house.

"Game ware very plentiful — thousands of prairie chickens and partridges and abundance of mink and deer. The streams ware full of pickerel, pike, and bass, and at first we just about lived on fish and what we shot. There was lots of beaver in the cricks, and the dams they made with their mud and moss was wonderful. I've seen popple trees a foot through they'd gnawed off. The popple ware the tree they seemed to like best; but they cut down willow and soft maple some too.

"There's game around here still; but it's been a good many years since I've had a first-class hunt. The last ware when a cousin of mine ware visitin' me. He 'n' his wife and me 'n' my wife hitched into a double express wagon and took our dinners and went after prairie chickens. It ware about the first of August. The young chickens are two-thirds grown then and are as nice eatin' as anythin' you could ask. We went out on the prairie, and then my cousin and I took our guns and commenced to walk. The ladies drove the team and follered us, and they'd keep track of where a covey lit. We had some good dogs, and we bagged a hundred and twenty chickens that day.

"When I settled here there was just one man in this region, and he had a cabin in the timber by the crick. But the emigrants ware arrivin' all the summer, and by winter we had a dozen families right around.

"Every spring and fall the Indians used to come here and stay a couple of weeks hunting and fishing. We never had no trouble with 'em until 1862. Then they made war, and for two hundred miles of the frontier they fell on the whites, and in thirty-six hours had killed nearly a thousand and took hundreds of prisoners. I don't know how the trouble began. Some say a party of Indians got drunk and murdered a man who refused to give 'em more whiskey, and that then they fled to their encampment, and the rest of the Indians decided to protect them. So they all went and started a massacree. Others say the Indians didn't get their rights from the government and ware neglected and ware paid their annuities in greenbacks instead of in gold or silver as had been the habit.

"Anyhow the Indians commenced to burn houses and to kill as many whites as they could. The people flocked here from a hundred miles back, and when the first refugees come I can tell you things did look scarry. We got ready every gun and all the ammunition in the place, and posted pickets. Some expected the Indians ware right behind follerin' of 'em. However, they didn't show up that night, and we didn't really know what they ware doin' of. So the next day we sent out scouts. They found the Indians had gone, and they haven't disturbed us in our part of the state since."

These reminiscences were related to me by Mr. Dobbs one afternoon while we sat in the shade of the trees on the plank bench in front of the hotel. The sun shone clear and hot on the dusty street. Three or four teams were hitched to posts and telegraph poles, and the horses stood half asleep patiently waiting for their masters. On the shadowed side of the street were a few men sitting on the stone steps or window ledges talking together or reading papers. On the sunny side the store curtains were pulled down to shut out the heat and glare. Business seemed to have come to a standstill, and in the depths of the leading grocery store I could hear the proprietor tooting on a cornet with amazing persistency.

None of the stores had signs, and I was informed that some stores had only been in business a few months and it was not time to expect them to get up signs; while the older ones were well known to everybody, and where was the need of their having signs?

On a corner across the way from the hotel was a one-man bank. When the village mail arrived the banker locked up while he leisurely visited the post-office. Next to the bank was what seemed to be a one-man store, and its proprietor, like the banker, went to the post-office; but he left his door wide open. He was a tall, round-shouldered man, with a leathery face and a brush of chin whiskers. His hat was a squatty derby of antique style, and his scant-lengthed trousers were patched on the seat. He was in his shirt sleeves and had his thumbs thrust into the armholes of his vest with an air of self-satisfied independence. In his window, amid a dubious array of merchandise, was a fly-specked card on which was stencilled the words

GOODS SOLD AT COST

I made inquiry about this sign and about his business. "He's an old-timer," I was told. "He was here before the flood, and he's been sellin' goods 'at cost' and makin' money ever since. He does most of his work himself, though he has a boy around to help when he can find him; but that's not often."

In the evening things grew busier, and now and then a buggy would arrive in a cloud of dust, and the street grew quite populous with teams and loitering people. Some trading was done, but more visiting. The men gathered in groups on the dim-lit walks before the stores and swore amiably at each other, as they chatted, by the hour together.

In what I saw of the region on my walks out into the surrounding country its aspect varied little. Whichever way I went I found smooth, straight dirt roads, and land flowing along endlessly with a hardly perceptible rise and fall. The staple crops raised in the great fields were corn, oats, and barley. Some wheat was grown; but the soil did not sustain it as well as formerly and it seldom does really well. Flax-growing, too, has been gradually abandoned for the same reason.

The farm dwellings were always among trees — often in one of the natural oak woods, or on the edge of it; but more commonly in the midst of a planted square of poplars, willows, and maples that enclosed all the buildings and the garden. Every man apparently aspired to have a big red barn with a gambrel roof and a cupola on top. There were pretty sure to be flowers and shrubbery near the house; but in the remoter portions of the yard was much litter, including a woodpile, wagons, tools, worn-out machinery, and some more or less depleted straw stacks. The dwellings as a whole had a pleasing look of prosperity and comfort.

The tillers of the soil are of many nationalities, and they show a strong tendency to gather in racial settlements. Thus, in one vicinity you will find all Germans, in another all Norse, and so on. If settlers of a particular race are at all numerous in a district they have their own church and church school, and in the school the text-books are mostly in the native language, though enough English is imparted to enable the children to speak and read it intelligently.

I stopped at a German home one noon for dinner. We ate in the hot, smudgy little kitchen close to the stove. There were three children in the family, two of them boys, and the other a tall attractive girl, who waited on the table — probably because there was not room for her to sit with the rest. We had fried ham, bread and butter, coffee and cake. German was the ordinary language of the household, and before we began to eat, each of the boys asked a blessing in that language. Dinner for the youngsters consisted mostly of bread plentifully bespread with molasses. Every time a lad finished pouring from the molasses pitcher he gave the nose of it a swipe with his tongue to prevent its dripping.

I asked the man if the Minnesota country suited him as well as his native Europe.

"Gosh, yes!" was the response; "but my woman complains about the cold long winter. It's a little bit too long. When I come twenty-seven years ago the land around here was owned by one man. He'd got a whole section, by golly, as a speculation. The land he sold me was covered with scrubby bushes and was so wet you couldn't walk anywhere without gettin' your boots or shoes filled with water. But cultivation and ditches has dried it off. About ten years ago I built this house and a new barn. I wa'n't goin' to live in an old shack all my life. I had to go in debt some, and that's the case with nearly all when they build; but most are gradually payin'."

After dinner we sat for a while in the parlor, which was impressively neat as the result of a recent house-cleaning. The gay rag carpet had just been put back on the floor, and there was straw beneath it which made it puff up like a cushion; but it would tread down flat in time.

"Do you think the government'll continue this rural delivery that they been extendin' everywhere?" queried my host; and he also wanted to know if the cost of the service fell on the farmers. "Some people here say it ain't a good thing," he continued. "They claim the expense is more'n it's worth. I ain't talkin' much myself, because my son-in-law runs the mail car, and I don't want him to lose his job."

Views as to the farm prosperity of the region differed widely. I had a chat with one man planting corn in a wayside field whose comments were decidedly pessimistic. "I bought my land in this blamed country when land was cheap," he said; "and yet it's been mighty hard work to pay for it. I don't know as I could have paid if I hadn't had money come to me from elsewhere. You see when a feller borrowed fifteen years ago he had to pay ten per cent interest. Now you get lower interest, but the price of land is up to fifty dollars or more an acre. Whoever buys at such a price will never pay any of the principal in the world.

"It's them Germans up north of the town who have raised the price of land here. The thing happened this way — some German in Wisconsin sold out sixty acres he had there for one hundred dollars an acre. That made six thousand dollars, and he come here lookin' for another farm. Well, he struck a Yankee man up north of the town who had one hundred and twenty acres and wanted to sell. They got talkin' same as you and me are now, and the German offered all his money for that farm and got it. After sellin' at a hundred dollars an acre, fifty dollars an acre looked cheap, and yet the Yankee had offered me the same farm the week before for thirty-five hundred dollars. Since that sale no one will dispose of any land for less than that Wisconsin feller paid. He made a mistake, but them Germans are good thrifty people and get rich if any one can. They keep things lookin' nice around the house, too. The German women have all got a flower garden, every last one of 'em.

"The Norse are thrifty, too. Yes, they're about as careful a lot of citizens as we have; but I don't like 'em. They're a high-toned sort of people and honest; and yet at the same time they're selfish and have kind of a darn mean way. They don't have to be here long from Europe before they're a little ashamed of being Norse. Soon as they learn to talk English they think they're a little better'n you are, and act as if they had an idea they knew a blamed sight more than any one else. They're great hands to put up big buildings, and once in a while one attempts a little more style than he can carry out.

"That's the trouble with most people here. They feel bound to put on style, and so are kept in debt. They buy fancy buggies and two-seated covered rigs and other things of the sort; not because they need 'em, but because some rich men they know have got such things. They buy expensive machinery, too; but they don't take care of it. A man'll invest sixty or seventy dollars in a gang plough; and the first season he'll put it in the shed, but the next year he'll leave it in the field just where he got through using it. Some of the machines they run under a bunch of trees when they ain't in use, and there they stay and rot. The shade keeps 'em from dryin' after a rain, and they're ruined. They'd be better off right out in the sun. Worse still, the people keep a miserable lot of stock of all kinds — horses, cattle, and everything else; and they turn 'em out to pasture in the spring as soon as the grass starts, and the cattle keep ahead of the grass the season through and ain't never really well fed. The buildings, too, are put up just as cheap as possible and won't last."

The sky had been growing threatening while we talked, and I now thought it best to start for town. On the way I encountered a little spatter of rain; but it was soon over, the clouds drifted on and streaks of sunshine glimmered across the vast landscape. When I arrived at the hotel office I found several people there driven in by the shower and in no hurry to depart as long as the conversation was interesting. One of the men was the landlord. He was as much a farmer as a hotel-keeper, and he was coatless and had on overalls. Another man was a house painter, who was complaining because a certain citizen would not give him the job of painting his buildings. When he came to a pause I spoke of my cornfield acquaintance and repeated some of his pessimistic remarks.

"That's straight," corroborated the painter. "A man can come here with six good horses to-day, and in a dozen years he won't have enough money to get out of the country. Suppose he takes land and farms it to halves; at the end of the season, after payin' expenses, the profits won't buy a bushel of potatoes. He'd be ten times better off to go up in the woods or on the railroad and work by the day."

"Now stop right thar!" said the landlord. "I've been here four times as long as you have, and I've farmed it, too, and I can tell you thar ain't a better country lays outdoors than southern Minnesota."

"That talk'll do for strangers," retorted the painter; "but, by gee! it won't do for me. My brother has got a quarter section here, and he'd starve to death if I didn't help him. Yes, sir, any renter who pays his rent and boards his family is doin' a darn big thing; and you can stand such a man on his head when he's through a season and you can't shake five dollars out of his pocket."

"Look here!" exclaimed the landlord, "the best land we got rents for two dollars an acre; and the man who can't make money on it ain't no farmer. Whar is your brother situated?"

"Four miles out on the east road."

"Oh, well, I ain't surprised now I know whar he is. That land is so cold and sour you couldn't raise quack grass on it."

The painter laughed and said: "A feller was tellin' me a quack grass story only yesterday. He claimed he lost his hat-band one summer day and he picked some quack grass and tied it around his hat. When he come in at night his wife took off the quack grass and put it in the fire, and not long afterward she emptied out the ashes from the stove, and within a few days there come up a lot of quack grass where she throwed them ashes."

"You can't kill it," affirmed the landlord, "and its sprouts have got such sharp, horny points that they'll go right through a potato, or even through a pine board. You can pull up a bunch of it and hang it on a fence post, and the next year throw it down and it'll grow."

"You bet your boots it will," said the painter.

"To show you what sort of a country this is," continued the landlord, "I'll tell you what I done last year. Thar was a part of my cornfield that I raised seventy bushels an acre on."

"Not much you didn't," disputed the painter. "Thirty bushels would be closeter to it."

"I maysured it," the landlord declared, "and I'll leave it to the feller that did the husking. You know Jack Searles. He did most the whole job for me at three cents and a half a bushel; and he'd do one hundred and fifty bushels in a day. He did everlastingly rip them ears out o' the husks. Why, me 'n' my hired man tried racin' with him, and we husked like cusses; but he did five bushels while both of us together was doin' two."

"Seventy bushels to an acre!" scoffed the painter.

"It can't be done. Must 'a' been something like an ear of corn I fixed up to show in a store window. I cut off the tip of one ear and the butt of another. The places where I cut just matched in size and I stuck a stiff piece of wire in the cobs and joined the two ears together. It looked like a single ear, and I'll be dog-goned if it wa'n't more'n three feet long. Your corn-field was down by the creek, wa'n't it?"

"Yes."

"I saw it a year ago just after the corn come up, and I never see such crooked rows before in my life."

"My man planted it," explained the landlord, "and I was tellin' him we'd have to use the same horse to cultivate we did to plant because none o' the others could go so crooked."

"Well," said the painter, "you must 'a' had to blind-fold the horse then to get it through some o' the rows."

"You can joke," remarked the landlord rather testily; "but I raised all the corn I said I did on that field. I can make money here, and so can others, though I will say, with the land at present prices, a man has to scratch and be a good manager to get to own it. But thar ain't one man in ten of our farmers in debt now, while twenty years ago not more'n one in ten was out of debt."

The discussion was beginning to wax hot again when one of the occupants of the room called us all to the window. A rusty, gray old man was walking past accompanying a pudgy old woman. He was very attentive, and there was a touch of gallantry and an attempt to make himself agreeable that was not to be mistaken.

"Gee whiz!" exclaimed the painter, "he's a widower and she's a widow."

"Yes," said another, "that's goin' to be a match sure! His son has just married her daughter, and now the old folks are goin' to hitch."

"He was pretty well discouraged after his wife died," said the painter. "If he was haulin' a load of straw and had a tipover, or if any other little thing didn't go right, he was ready to leave this forsaken country. But he seems to have chirked up and I s'pose everything is lovely."

"If that don't beat the Dutch!" commented the landlord.

The dispute about the prosperity of the region had been forgotten; for this glimpse of romance had been like oil on troubled waters.

NOTE. — Any characteristic portion of our country repays acquaintance, and the prairie lands of southern Minnesota are no exception. They are monotonous, and the tourist may not be tempted to linger long, but that should not hinder getting a sample experience. Hotels in the smaller places are often rude, but rarely are actually uncomfortable, and the food, if not fine, is palatable. The country itself is in some of its aspects really beautiful, the life with its varied mixtures of peoples from Europe is interesting, and the impressions you gain have lasting value.

BASIC FACTS

Capital City	St. Paul
Nickname	The North Star State
Flower	Pink and White Lady's-Slipper
Bird	Common Loon
Tree	Red Pine
Song	*Hail! Minnesota*
Gemstone	Lake Superior Agate
Fish	Walleye
Entered the Union	May 11, 1858

STATISTICS*

Land Area (square miles)	79,289
Rank in Nation	14th
Population†	3,877,000
Rank in Nation	19th
Density per square mile	48.9
Number of Representatives in Congress	8
Capital City	St. Paul
Population	309,866
Rank in State	2nd
Largest City	Minneapolis
Population	434,400
Number of Cities over 10,000 Population	53
Number of Counties	87

---

* Based on 1970 census statistics compiled by the Bureau of the Census.

† Estimated by Bureau of the Census for July 1, 1972.

MAP OF CONGRESSIONAL DISTRICTS OF MINNESOTA

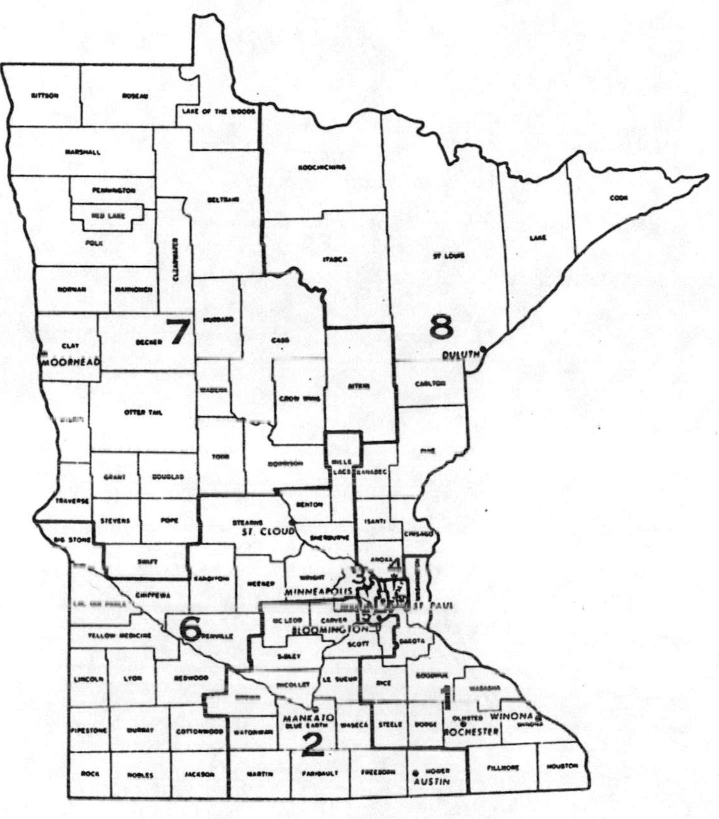

MAP OF CONGRESSIONAL DISTRICTS OF MINNESOTA

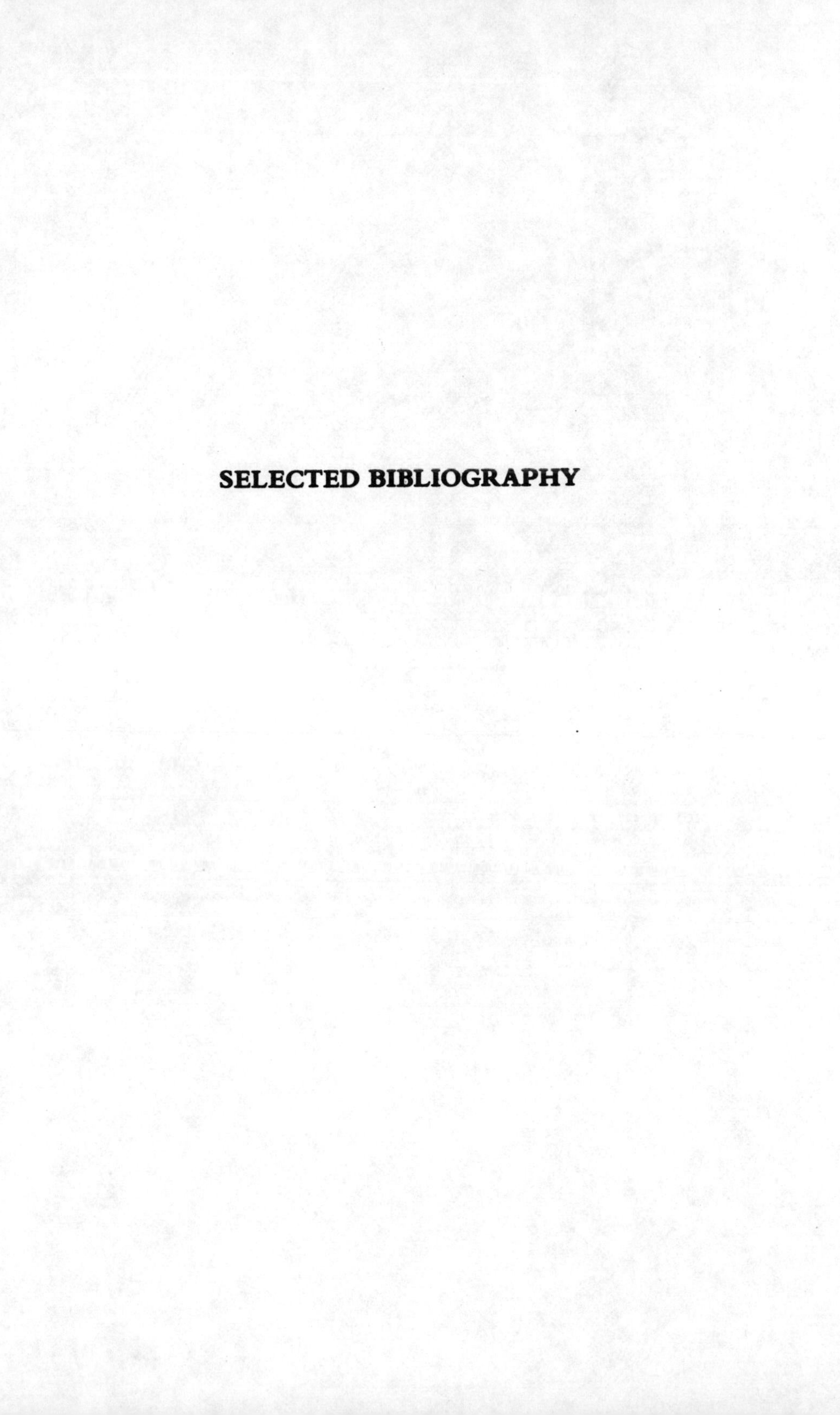

SELECTED BIBLIOGRAPHY

Blegen, Theodore Christian. Minnesota; A History of the State. Minneapolis: University of Minnesota Press, 1963

Brings, Lawrence Martin. Minnesota Heritage: A Panoramic Narrative. Minneapolis: T. S. Denison, 1960

Burnquist, Joseph Alfred Arner, ed. Minnesota and Its People. 4 vols. Chicago: The S. J. Clarke Publishing Co., 1924

Castle, Henry Anson. Minnesota, Its Story and Biography. 3 vols. Chicago and New York: The Lewis Publishing Company, 1915.

Cheyney, Edward Gheen. The Birth of the North Land. Cloquet, Minn.: The Northwest Paper Co., 1933.

Christianson, Theodore. Minnesota, The Land of Sky-tainted Waters, A History of the State and Its People. 5 vols. Chicago and New York: The American Historical Society, Inc., 1935.

Flandrau, Charles Eugene. The History of Minnesota and Tales of the Frontier. St. Paul: E. W. Porter, 1900.

Gilman, Rhodee R. and J. D. Holmquist, eds. Minnesota History: Selections. Minneapolis, 1965.

Heilborn, Bertha Lion. The Thirty-Second State: A Pictorial History of Minnesota. 2nd ed. St. Paul: Minnesota Historical Society, 1966.

Jones, Evan. Citadel in the Wilderness: Fort Snelling and Old Northwest Frontier. New York: Coward-McCann, 1966.

Kunz, Virginia (Brainard). Muskets to Missiles: Military History of Minnesota. St. Paul: Minnesota Statehood Centennial Commission, 1958.

Le Sueur, Meridel. North Star Country. New York: Duell, Sloan and Pearce, 1945

Lindquist, Maude Lucille and James W. Clark. Community Life in Minnesota. New York: C. Scribner's Sons, 1933.

Mayo, Robert J. Adventures in Minnesota History. Milwaukee, Minneapolis: E. M. Hale and Co., 1931.

Nute, Grace Lee. Rainy River Country; A Brief History of the Region Bordering Minnesota and Ontario. St. Paul: Minnesota Historical Society, 1950.

____________. Voyageur's Highway: Minnesota's Border Lake Land. St. Paul: The Minnesota Historical Society, 1941.

Painter, Clara Searle and Anne Brezler. Minnesota Grows Up. Minneapolis: The University of Minnesota Press, 1936.

Parsons, E. Dudley. The Story of Minnesota. New York: American Book Company, 1916.

NAME INDEX